THE AMERICAN DREAM
A GUIDE FOR IMMIGRANTS AND VISITORS

With this Guide, the authors have shared their knowledge and love for America so readers and visitors alike could profit from their experience and participate in American society and culture more easily and fully. "To Know America is loving her," say the authors. Dr. D'Souza's own love affair with America started 42 years ago when he left Mangalore, India to pursue higher studies.

Whether you are just visiting, pursuing business opportunities, or your education in the United States, this Guide contains useful practical advice to make your stay in the United States more productive and enjoyable.

Written especially for students, business people, visitors, and émigrés this Guide contains valuable information that will open doors to understanding and appreciation of American Society, culture, business, and education thus increasing your chances of achieving success in the United States of America.

The
American
Dream

Arthur D'Souza

authorHOUSE®

AuthorHouse™
1663 Liberty Drive
Bloomington, IN 47403
www.authorhouse.com
Phone: 1-800-839-8640

First published by AuthorHouse   3/16/2011

ISBN: 978-1-4490-6796-0 (sc)
ISBN: 978-1-4567-1400-0 (e)

THE AMERICAN DREAM
DISCOVER AMERICA

YOUR HANDBOOK TO SUCCESS IN AMERICA

PURSUE

YOUR

DREAM

Read this Guide to become familiar with American way of living. Dress, behave, and interact with Americans appropriately as this Guide describes and increase your chances for success.

Avoid cultural faux paux!

You may be the most wonderful person in the world but unless you convey it to people around you and to all those you meet, it will not matter how wonderful you are! Regardless of what you really are or what you think of yourself, others can only know the real you by the way you look, dress, behave, interact, and communicate. You project the "real you" by your actions and behavior for all to see and experience.

ACKNOWLEDGEMENTS

The planning, writing and publication of this Guide is made possible by so many well-wishers and friends that a complete account of individual contributions is impossible. The conception, execution, and organization of useful information in the form of a Guide are a true accomplishment. In this context I would like to thank the following contributors who made time and effort amidst their busy schedules to assist me in this undertaking.

The co-author Ken Brand and his wife Marilyn Brand took upon themselves to conceive and design the manuscript. Their personal experience with several foreign students and acquaintances made their contributions so valuable.

Dr. John Cimprich (professor, Department of History, Thomas More College) graciously offered his comments. His perspective and suggestions greatly helped to depict historical events and avoid folklore.

The editor of this Guide, Phil Paradis helped to produce a truly objective, reader-friendly Guide. His efforts to incorporate American English into this Guide were appreciated.

My wonderful family, without whose unlimited patience, helpful suggestions, enthusiastic support, and encouragement this project would have been impossible to accomplish.

Ameer Ullal for his superb computer support throughout the preparation of this manuscript.

PROLOGUE
SEIZING THE AMERICAN DREAM

A TRUE STORY

After months of anxiety and excitement on a bright sunny day of September 1967, I boarded an Air India flight in Mumbai, destination New York. My brother, equally anxious and excited about my arrival to the United States, met me at the JFK International airport terminal. We exchanged brotherly love, reminisced good old village life in Mangalore, India. Then we started our long journey to Cincinnati, Ohio. The journey was tiresome yet pleasant. The scenic highway ride to Cincinnati through the plains, mountains, tunnels, vast corn fields, and wide open blue skies kept me awake!

It was 42 years ago. This was the first time I ventured away from my home in Mangalore. My skills were limited or at best useless in the new environment. Cooking, housekeeping, shopping, and other chores were totally new to me. The customs of United States and people seemed strange. English language with American accent was totally Greek to me! Yet I needed to overcome these deficiencies in order to achieve my goals. This opportunity of a lifetime must not be wasted.

The choice was simple yet tough. My determination to make this dream a reality and to become a success in the United States actually motivated me to work and study hard. For my good fortune I met several fine families and friends in Cincinnati who showed great love and interest in me. They taught me the social skills, proper etiquettes, and above all the fine intricacies of American way of life.

During my undergraduate and graduate studies I worked for multiple hospital laboratories. This experience was helpful in securing my first full time job as a Research Associate at University of Cincinnati Medical Center upon graduation. However my heart was set on owning my own business, a clinical diagnostic laboratory. Just a few years later I was able to pool my resources and establish Cincinnati Medical Laboratory. Many of my loyal friends and large number of acquaintances applauded my efforts and wholeheartedly supported my laboratory any which way they could. Some of them became my clients. These clients referred my services to others they knew - helping me increase and expand my laboratory sales into a multi-million dollar venture within a short period of 6-8 years. Cincinnati Med-Lab was well recognized as a leader and an exceptional quality service provider by area clinics, nursing homes, and physicians.

The secret for this unusual success is simple – work hard, meet people, make friends, and painstakingly maintain friendships and commitments. My long journey to the United States, rare glimpses of success, and many failures is my story! There are thousands of real life American stories such as this. Many of them are more interesting and heart-warming than this! Good luck, happy reading, and...... you may too become a success in the good old United States of America.

CONTENTS

THE AMERICAN DREAM

INTRODUCTION

When I visit schools and colleges in my hometown, Mangalore, India, I am deluged with questions such as "what is America like? what are Americans like?, how do they live?, are they nice and friendly?" The excitement and intrigue is evident in the voice of these tender hearts! Many students also inquire about the system of education, ways to secure admission to colleges, universities, and of course employment opportunities in the United States.

United States is world's favorite destination for students, visitors, professionals, and entrepreneurs. Most new arrivals to the United States quickly adapt, learn, and continue to make progress but some new arrivals are slow to learn and adapt. Everyday living in the United States consists of chores such as shopping, cooking, cleaning, laundry, not to mention homework, house work, and social obligations. A disillusioned, discouraged new arrival most likely may hang his hat and leave!

Most of these talented men and women would move heaven and earth to land in the United States - the land of hope and opportunity.

They come with high hopes and a burning desire to succeed in the United States. All fatigued nervous visitors as they line up at the port of entry can barely hide their excitement. This is the dreamland they have heard and read so much about. It is only a few steps away. A few more steps and America will be in sight! They have a mission and a vision. They are prepared to work hard, explore opportunities, and give all they have in order to achieve their idea of the great American Dream.

Most new arrivals not only accomplish their goals but excel beyond their own expectations. We have studied many of them in the hope of discovering some common denominators so that you may benefit from our research. We point out however that this Guide may present a "one size fits all" approach. Just like individuals are never all alike nor should a recipe for your success be!

Yet some find themselves wanting. They are interested and self-assured, yet fail. Why? Those who failed in their pursuit to excel may have faced great obstacles, lacked priorities, had false hopes, or simply missed their opportunities. In many cases it's not the level of intelligence or self confidence that causes failure but the individual's lack of clear priorities and knowledge of the true American spirit. Some immigrants to the United States may not have prepared themselves adequately to face the challenges and overcome difficulties they may encounter. This Guide is written for you - an interested individual who has a desire to immigrate to the United States, willing to adapt, accept the challenge, learn the ropes, achieve your cherished goals, and fulfill your dreams. This Guide will certainly increase your knowledge, understanding, appreciation of America, her people, culture, customs, and above all - that great American spirit! In the nutshell we show you the way, prepare you well, reinforce you adequately so you can seize the opportunities at hand and apply your learned skills to succeed.

We have analyzed the problems faced by unsuccessful individuals to develop this Guide. We have found some common behaviors and situations among those who have had problems that impeded their progress and chances for success in the United States. The purpose of this Guide is to identify those problems so that you may learn from them. In these pages we share many pitfalls that others have faced so you may avoid them. We list and describe them plainly, concisely, and bluntly. We encourage you to learn, understand, and apply our recommended techniques to your own routine life in the United States. The positive behaviors we list will enhance not only your business and professional endeavors but also your associations, friendships, social skills, and personal life. We propose many concrete, proven methods you should follow to succeed. This Guide is designed for those who are willing to learn from mistakes others have made. Following a step-by-step approach, common sense, adaptation to new way of living to overcome some of the difficult situations outlined in this Guide can help you achieve the impossible!

We speak of failures only to bring out the obvious - that true success is possible for those who are willing to listen, learn, and adapt to American spirit and culture. Talented professionals, savvy investors, educators, and intellectuals must know that United States has its own unique blend of culture and subcultures. Understanding and practicing American culture and spirit requires skill and interest. The message to learn and adapt to variety of situations is clear. Therefore we suggest that you become familiar with American culture, customs, and spirit before you land in the United States - that would make a big difference. However there is no way this Guide, any book or any set of books will give you an understanding of the total complexity of the whole Americanism. The most effective way to learn and understand the American way of life is by living in the United States. Like any other country in the world, United States has its own national identity, way of life, unique culture, and myriad subcultures. Your adaptation to and eventual integration into American society will be a huge admirable achievement! We admit that the cultural diversity of the United States can make your head spin. But do not despair!

We present this Guide from our personal experience. You must understand that all situations you will encounter are not alike. Some may be identical and others may bear some similarities. Take time and make effort to understand people you deal with, respond appropriately, and respectfully. Your success depends upon how well you deal with, respond to, and address these unique encounters. Therefore we suggest that this Guide be viewed in its entirety and with proper perspective.

A Sense Of America And What America Is All About:

America is an open society. The government of the United States of America was established over 200 years ago. America's founding fathers envisioned a society free of fear, oppression, prejudice, and discrimination. The primary function of the government was to allow citizens to pursue their dreams and happiness. Individuals with talent, ambition, drive, and motivation may freely engage in endeavors of their choice and achieve success through determination and hard work.

United States is a land of opportunity for all. It's also known as the "melting pot" of the world. Your national origin, race, religion, skin color, and gender will hardly affect or influence your chances for success. Believe it or not your success will depend upon you! Through your actions and behaviors you mold and create your future. In a capitalistic cum open society, success comes to those who are creative and willing to work hard. Your own innovative and futuristic approach will determine the measure of your success. The American free market economy, the engine of capitalism will allow you to achieve your high goals you set for yourself.

United States is the most affluent country in the world. America has abundant natural resources, wide open fertile plains, and miles of pristine shoreline. Among all industrialized nations, United States has the most diverse and affluent society. This is largely due to the Industrial Revolution, modern technology, and the solid work ethics of American workforce. Whether it's manufacturing, agriculture, health, sciences or any other field, United States is second to none. United States has the advantage of a free enterprise economy that attracts individuals, private businesses, and savvy investors from all over the world. You are free to work, establish and operate a business of your choice wherever you desire. It's little wonder therefore United States is a favorite destination to so many businessmen and women.

The friendly, open, and tolerant society of United States is a matter of national pride. The society as a whole has cultivated respect for individual, religious, and political freedom. In communities and neighborhoods across America you will find people of different ethnicity, religion, color, stature, educational level, personal values, and behaviors living in peace and harmony. This diversity is America's greatest strength which has fostered family values, tolerance, and a unique blend of true Americanism.

It's true that United States is not perfect just as there is no place on earth that has ever been perfect. United States has social problems, crime, corruption, prejudice, and many other ills just like all other countries of the world! Yet, when compared to those countries United States stands tall and proud for what it is and the noble ideals it stands for. All U.S. citizens enjoy freedom of speech, religious freedom, individual liberties, and investment opportunities as guaranteed by the constitution. The government of the United States is freely elected by the people, of the people, and for the people. The United States' constitution guarantees that the government will not interfere with your right to life, liberty, and the pursuit of happiness. The United States' constitution is set up to protect your individual rights and freedom rather than to control you, dictate to you, and deny them to you. The U.S. constitution's 5th Amendment says "No person shall... be deprived of life, liberty, or property, without due process of law." This guarantee is the American ideal that attracts people from all over the globe to its shores. Millions of immigrants who embraced United States as their new home away from home have worked hard to make this country one of the most affluent and powerful on the face of the earth and in return they have been abundantly rewarded.

As you land in the United States a multitude of challenges await you. Apartment hunting, transportation, shopping, cooking, and above all getting familiar with the place and people! This is no easy task by any standards! Good communication skills, social etiquettes, and respect for all people you deal with are critically important. Americans by and large are quite accommodating and sympathetic to new immigrants. Many of them have had your experience firsthand not so long ago!

Most Americans are exceptionally friendly and supportive. Make sure that you deal with them fairly and truthfully. Try to learn American English as soon as possible and as well as possible. As you overcome any shyness and communication barriers, life for you in the United States will become easier and easier. You will love your new-found home like no other!

You will notice the use of phrases, idioms, and clichés much too frequently in American homes, places of work, worship, and study. The phrases and idioms have no literal meaning yet used in the right context they convey a powerful message, demands, advice, humor, and the like. You will find such phrases and idioms used throughout this

Guide. We have compiled a list of such clichés, idioms, and phrases for your reference in a separate chapter.

We suggest individuals who plan to visit United States be familiar with the true American spirit and American way of life. The message and mantra of this Guide is to prepare you by providing a preview of the real thing! This Guide will serve as your resource if you plan to study, work, visit, and invest in the United States. You prepare yourself to meet your life's challenges head-on, anticipate the next turn, cliff, slope, or hoop you may have to make. We guide you all the way! Rather than being unaware and blindfolded, this Guide will educate and enlighten you. We recommend this Guide to special categories of aspiring immigrants listed below:

- Au pairs and Students who wish to pursue higher studies.
- Professionals such as computer specialists, engineers, physicians, scientists, and technicians.
- Educators (teachers, scientists, professors).
- Entertainers, musicians, performers.
- Entrepreneurs, investors, businessmen and women.
- Visitors, tourists, and nature lovers.
- Refugees and Asylum seekers (asylees).

In order to provide additional information to you, we have developed a separate resource section - the Appendix. Appendix will provide valuable information for immigrants, students, visitors, and all those who plan to visit United States. America's world famous educational institutions, museums, tourist attractions, natural wonders, and man-made wonders are all listed so you will not miss out on history and treasures of this great nation. There is something for everyone!

Most temporary or permanent immigrants seldom experience any inconvenience at the point of entry to the United States. Yet on occasion some may find themselves bombarded with questions by the customs officers, security, and other law enforcement agents. If by random chance you encounter such a situation as unpleasant it may be, answer all questions truthfully. You may be asked about your programs, intentions, duration of your stay, people you know, and a list of places you will visit. Remember that you are on American soil and you have all the rights and privileges of an American citizen. Exercise your rights – respond to all queries truthfully, candidly, consistently, and respectfully.

American's outlook on foreigners has dramatically changed since 9/11. Upon your arrival at the port of entry, you may be questioned, detained, and delayed by the customs officers for whatever reason or suspicion they may have. You may even be searched. You have every right to be silent, to request a lawyer, and "protect" yourself. Only a judge may order you to answer questions. However it is wise to cooperate and answer all questions truthfully. Address every concern of law enforcement agent(s) with utmost care. If language is a barrier, request an interpreter in order to make your case fully. It's likely that you were randomly selected for an elaborate, comprehensive search as part of the routine Homeland Security Procedure. For the safety of fellow travellers and general public these extraordinary security measures are necessary. Your whole-hearted cooperation and compliance is vital for the national security of the United States.

CHAPTER ONE
UNITED STATES OF AMERICA – A BRIEF HISTORY

American Presidents And Important Events

History Of The American Flag

"..give me your tired, your poor,
Your huddled masses yearning to breathe free,
The wretched refuse of your teeming shore.
Send these, the homeless, tempest-tost to me,
I lift my lamp beside the golden door!"
-Emma Lazarus, "The New Colossus" – 1883.

Amerigo Vespucci, an Italian merchant explorer claimed to have discovered "the new world" in 1497. The Americas, the American continents - North and South were named after Amerigo. Christopher Columbus discovered the western hemisphere in 1492, but wrongly believed it to be the orient! Columbus is honored for this discovery with many monuments in countries of South America and also in the United States. Columbus Day, a legal federal holiday is celebrated on the second Monday in October with marches, parades, and picnics throughout the United States.

American history is the story of a great wilderness tamed and modernized in a matter of less than 500 years. The nation is built on the principle that all individuals have a right to "life, liberty, and the pursuit of happiness." The history of ancient civilizations is filled with the stories of kings and emperors. American history is mostly an account of millions of Europeans who left their native lands to seek economic opportunity, avoid religious persecution or political oppression. This Guide deals with the North American continent that became the United States of America (USA) but much of it also applies to Canada.

Original American natives, the Indian tribes lived on this vast land for thousands of years. The Indians soon lost their land and much more as more and more European migrants arrived. The Europeans crossed the Atlantic Ocean in the early 1500's. The first organized permanent English settlement in America was established in 1607 in Jamestown, Virginia. It was named after King James I of England. Jamestown's settlers numbered less than a thousand conceived and set up the first representative assembly in America under the Virginia Charter prepared by the king. The charter or a commission of privileges, orders, and laws that proclaimed "this great charter is to bind us and our heirs forever...." To have a voice and a vote in the colony's affairs one had to own a small amount of land, belong to the Anglican Church, and be an adult male.

The famous Mayflower soon arrived with Pilgrims in November 1620, landed in coastal Massachusetts, and built their own settlement. The men on the ship drafted an early American constitution. In the early 1600's more British made the voyage in search of freedom and treasure. Other Europeans who followed and landed on the Atlantic coast also lived in the colonies. French, Germans, Irish, Dutch, and Spaniards rushed to the new world after the British. Most of them settled along the eastern coastal regions and some migrated inland in search of fertile land. By 1763, the British gained supremacy over lands that now comprise the eastern Atlantic Coast by defeating French in the famous French and Indian War (1754-1763). Then the British began to clamp down on the colonists in their effort to exploit the spoils of victory. The Stamp Tax Act of 1765 stirred up the first major resistance. The Townshend Duties of 1767 on British goods provoked colonists to organize the famous Boston Tea Party. The colonists much used to their freedom and autonomy, resisted repeated British encroachment on their liberties. They resented new taxation by the Empire. During this time there was no central government in North America. Every colony was a separate, independent, sovereign unit. The English colonists had established self-governance and initiated rule of law under separate royal charters.

Then the thirteen colonies banded together and fought the War of Independence or Revolutionary War that began on April 19, 1775 at Lexington and then at Concord near Boston, Massachusetts. The colonists lost ground at the famous battle of Bunker Hill but maintained their siege lines at Boston. The Revolutionary War continued under the able leadership of General George Washington. Yet the movement for independence was not going anywhere! In early 1776, the Independence movement got a shot in the arm from Thomas Paine, a British writer, who in his pamphlet "Common Sense" argued that Americans had not only the opportunity to bring about a free, happy democratic and progressive nation but had every right to do so. The Continental Congress voted for Independence on July 2, 1776 and adopted the Declaration of Independence on July 4, 1776. America was still at war and the War was not going well for the colonists. In the absence of a professional army, Commander George Washington and his generals were forced to fall back on untrained, inexperienced men. However the tide began to turn against the British when the United States and France signed an alliance on February 6, 1778. The war continued with both sides well entrenched and then America's hope re-ignited when French troops joined the fight and helped force the surrender of Lord Cornwallis' army to George Washington at Yorktown, Virginia, on Oct. 19, 1781.

The British withdrew from major battle zones and signed a preliminary peace treaty on November 30, 1782. The war formally ended with the Treaty of Paris on September 3, 1783. The treaty provided for liberal boundaries for America extending from the Atlantic Coast to the Mississippi River and from the Great Lakes to the 31st parallel in the South. The British left New York on November 25, 1783. American casualties for Revolutionary War included approximately 25,000 dead and an unknown number of men wounded.

United States had no duly elected central government even after hard fought Independence! The new government had no real authority to control trade and impose taxes. It was dependent on the states for budget and income. The 13 original colonies or states were sovereign. The state of Virginia played a pivotal role in getting the delegates from five states to attend a discourse on interstate commerce in Sept. 1786. The delegates of this Annapolis convention laid the groundwork for a larger and more inclusive convention of all 13 colonial states the following year. In 1787, a group of 55 men from 12 states (Rhode Island abstained) met in Independence Hall, Philadelphia, on May 14. They debated the concept of a stronger national government to gain obedience from all the states and respect abroad. The delegates, with George Washington presiding, produced one of the most important political documents ever written: The United States Constitution. Of the 55 delegates present only 39 stayed to the end to approve and witness the signing of the Constitution, the supreme law of the land. The new Constitution had its vocal critics and loyal supporters. Critics demanded adequate protection of individual liberties against possible encroachment by the new federal government. James Madison proposed 12 amendments to the Constitution. Congress approved them on Sept. 25, 1789. The amendments became effective on Dec. 15, 1791. These 12 amendments to the U.S. Constitution are collectively known as "The Bill of Rights."

The new Federal government headed by George Washington took office in the spring of 1789. Washington was elected President unanimously. A census taken in 1790, registered 4,000,000 persons living in the 13 original colonies of the United States of America.

Alexander Hamilton, the first secretary of the Treasury showed extraordinary courage and skill. He established the national mint and federal responsibility for relinquishing the national debt. He also persuaded Congress to pass laws to encourage manufacturing goods in the United States. When some people in western Pennsylvania rioted in response to new taxes on distilleries, Hamilton was instrumental in convincing President Washington to take firm measures to suppress "The Whisky Rebellion." As a consequence the Washington administration gained credibility. The integrity of the federal government was preserved and gained trust among citizens.

George Washington
First President Of United States Of America
And Father Of Our Nation

The federal government under George Washington and successive presidents made great strides in preserving the union. George Washington retired from the presidency in 1797. Vice President John

Adams succeeded George Washington as the young democracies' second President. John Adams was the first president to live in the White House. He guided the United States through some of its serious difficulties. By 1800, America's population had increased to 5,000,000 people. The United States also had a new capital - Washington D.C.

Thomas Jefferson won the presidency in 1800, and for the next eight years United States patiently avoided conflicts in Europe. Jefferson also fostered national unity. He is best known as the author of the Declaration of Independence and the founder of the Democratic Party. Thomas Jefferson earned fame as a diplomat and a political thinker. He also had wide range of interests and talents yet hardly any appetite for power!

James Madison who succeeded Jefferson became impatient with on-going conflicts in Europe. The country engaged in the war of 1812, famously known as the "needless war." He asked Congress to declare war against Great Britain on June 1, 1812. Congress passed the war resolution on June 18, 1812. The war ended with the Treaty of Ghent on Dec. 24, 1814. The last battle of the war, the Battle of New Orleans, also known as a needless battle was fought on Jan. 8, 1815, weeks after the peace treaty was signed! The War of 1812 settled none of the issues over which it was supposedly fought. However in the end it had united the country like never before. The patriotic fervor gave birth to the American national anthem: "The Star Spangled Banner" by Francis Scott Key.

James Monroe, the 5th President of United States brought in an era of good feeling. The country was not at war nor interested in political discord. The famous Monroe Doctrine also served notice on European nations not to interfere in the affairs of the republics in the western hemisphere.

America's 7th President Andrew Jackson was credited for emphasizing democracy and preserving the union. His slogan "Let the People Rule" made him popular. However his feud with the Second National Bank caused economic chaos and depression. Hundreds of businesses and banks collapsed, wages and prices fell, and the misery index rose to alarming heights. The young democracy weathered some severe storms during these years yet has survived the test of time!

The United States witnessed the great Industrial Revolution in the early 1800's. Improved transportation, industrial development coupled with reform movements pushed the nation to the forefront as a world power. Robert Fulton's steamer Clermont started operation on the Hudson River in 1807. By 1820, over 60 steamboats were traveling the Hudson and Mississippi rivers. By 1846, river commerce was nearly twice as much as United States' foreign trade.

While canals assisted commerce with transportation by water, locomotives moved manufactured goods by land. Train service for goods and passengers was established by 1835. Train travel was available to many cities in the north and mid-west. By 1850, more cities were added with better service.

The Industrial Revolution dramatically changed the pace and process of manufacturing goods. Elias Howe's invention, the sewing machine saved time, labor, and tremendously increased production. The textile industry that required enormous manual labor began using high output machinery. Foundries and steel mills were set up to meet the increased demands of industry for tools and machinery. The all-round rapid industrial growth brought a huge surge in wealth.

Along with Industrial Revolution came higher demand for factory hands. Though a substantial work force was available, a still greater labor force was needed to meet the acute demands. Between 1840 and 1850, over a million laborers arrived from Ireland alone!

American history is full of conflicts either at home or abroad. The

United States started the Mexican War over disputed territory of Texas. The Texan revolt of 1835 against the Mexican government set the stage. President James Polk, who was in favor of acquiring Texas and adjoining territories declared war on Mexico on May 13, 1846. Mexico was defeated in the war and also suffered heavy loss of life. The United States too lost many men. The American death toll in the Mexican war was 12,876. The War was concluded with a peace treaty on Feb. 2, 1848. United States acquired more than 525,000 square miles of new territory! The states of Arizona, California, Nevada, New Mexico, and Utah were formed out of this newly conquered land.

The Industrial Revolution brought with it demands for reform. One such burning issue was slavery. Since the early 1800's, many people in the North considered slavery to be inhumane and degrading. The plantations in the South were entirely dependent on the slave field labor and the South was determined to fight tooth and nail to maintain the status quo. The whole nation was tragically divided over this highly emotional issue. By 1840, the slavery issue had reached critical proportions and tempers were running high between North and South. The famous antislavery novel titled Uncle Tom's Cabin (1851) by Harriet B. Stowe added more fuel to the fire.

Abraham Lincoln was elected president in 1860. The South did not trust him to respect slavery. The brewing discontent erupted into a full-scale civil war on April 12, 1861. The Southern army attacked Fort Sumter in the harbor of Charleston, South Carolina. As the escalation continued, the Northern Union army fought back. The civil war continued relentlessly for the next 4 years. The confederate President Jefferson Davis had appointed Robert Edward Lee as a full general. When the Confederate General Joseph E. Johnston was wounded on May 31, 1862, Robert E. Lee was appointed Commander General of the confederate army. The confederate army had a few successes against the massive Northern Union armies. However in the battle of Gettysburg, Commander Robert Lee's generals were defeated. This was the turning point of the conflict. The civil war finally ended on April 9, 1865, with General Robert E. Lee's surrender to General Ulysses S. Grant at Appomattox Court House, Virginia. The civil war death toll to the Union army was 364,511 while the Confederate army lost 258,821 men.

The Civil War was a sad chapter in the history of United States. But it settled several issues for the good of the country. President Lincoln issued his famous Emancipation Proclamation on Jan. 1, 1863, that declared slaves to be free in the states that were still in rebellion. The Civil War clearly brought an end to inhumane slavery. The issue of secession of states from the Union was resolved once for all. No state has since opted nor contemplated to break away from the union!

The Civil War literally destroyed millions of American lives. Countless homes, buildings, and factories were burnt to the ground. Property loss was astronomical! The Congress passed several measures to rebuild the war torn economy. The taxes were raised to pay for the War. The Homestead Act of 1862 catalyzed a rapid growth of agriculture and agro-industries.

Lincoln also won a bitterly contested second term for office. In his second inaugural address to the nation, Lincoln pleaded for a kindly peace, "with malice toward none, with charity for all." He urged, "let us press forward to bind up the nation's wounds." But Lincoln was assassinated by southern conspirators on April 14, 1865, and Congress made only modest efforts to appease the South. Yet American Industry was strong and growing. Employees earned good wages. By 1900, the United States had become one of the greatest economic powers of the world. The population had surged to 75,000,000 people.

Reconstruction followed Civil War. The southern economy was in ruins and needed massive aid. The North was in no mood to help the battered South. Congressional Republicans were intent on reform and punishment. President Andrew Johnson, who succeeded Lincoln, fought the Republican Congress over this serious national tragedy. Angry Republican Congress retaliated, impeached, and even tried President Johnson! However the Senate acquitted him by one vote.

Ulysses Grant, the 18th president preached peace for the war torn country but pursued inconsistent policies. Federal Government controlled by Republican administrations exerted undue pressure over the South through Republican state governments. This was occasionally supported by a small post war United States' army. Violent resistance by Southern Democrats caused the demise of Republican controlled southern state governments. Public opinion in the North turned against the use of the army to support Republican rule as well. As a consequence President Rutherford Hayes allowed the struggling Republican state governments in Louisiana, South Carolina, and Florida to collapse.

The country as a whole with the exception of the South saw a great influx of wealth. Mark Twain called the post-civil war period "The Gilded Age" because of America's seemingly extravagant wealth. The rise of "Big Business" was greatly responsible for this phenomenon. Great businessmen like Cornelius Vanderbilt (1794-1877), Andrew Carnegie (1835-1919), and John D. Rockefeller (1839-1937) contributed heavily to conceive and grow Big Business!

Cornelius Vanderbilt was an ambitious young man. He owned and operated a ferryboat from Staten Island to New York City at age 16! By 1850, he was a leading steamship owner in the United States. He operated steamships to several U.S. ports and Europe. He also owned railroad lines that provided service from New York City to as far west as Chicago. Cornelius Vanderbilt pioneered the development of the nation's transport system.

Andrew Carnegie came to the United States from Scotland when he was just 13 years of age. He worked in a factory with a weekly wage of $1.20. The young Carnegie became a telegraph operator at the age of only 17. His next job as a railroad clerk lasted for a short time. He was quickly promoted as division manager for the company at the age of 24! Carnegie made his millions in the iron and steel business. He established several steel plants and in 1899, merged his interests into the Carnegie Steel Company, one of the largest industrial enterprises in the United States at the time.

John D. Rockefeller, son of a peddler worked as a clerk for a small produce firm at age 16. He invested his meager savings to form a partnership in a grain commission house. He saved the profits to venture into the oil business at age 23!

Rockefeller worked hard to organize and develop the oil business. He brought innovation, efficiency and centralized control to the industry. He established the Standard Oil Company in 1870 that controlled the flow of oil products to consumers. By the end of 1870's, Standard Oil Company owned refineries in Cleveland, New York City, Pittsburgh, and Philadelphia. By 1882, Rockefeller controlled almost all U.S. oil refining, distribution, and most of the world's oil trade. John D. Rockefeller was once the world's richest man.

The swift rise of big business also encouraged worker abuse and blatant discrimination. Workers under the leadership of Samuel Gompers formed the American Federation of Labor in 1886. The main goal of the union was to protect and safeguard workers' interests. Leaders of the American Federation of Labor worked to improve working and living conditions for all the union members. John Mitchell, president of the United Mine Workers of America led the first successful coal miners' strike in 1902. The mine workers were granted better pay and shorter work hours!

President James Garfield, who followed Hayes, was assassinated in July 1881. Vice president Chester Arthur succeeded Garfield. President Arthur introduced badly needed civil service reform. Congress passed the first Civil Service Reform Act, also known as Pendleton Civil Service Act. The first Civil Service Commission was also set up under this act that awarded more Federal Government jobs to capable individuals. Political affiliation was no longer a requirement for securing government employment!

Grover Cleveland, the first Democrat to be elected president after the Civil War, believed in honest government. He adopted the slogan "Public office is a public trust." He restored the public trust in government while in office. He lost a re-election bid to Benjamin Harrison but regained the Presidency four years later. Grover Cleveland is the only American president ever to serve two non-consecutive terms!

The United States, as a world power found itself in yet another conflict with the Cuban crisis of 1898. Spanish misrule of Cuba was a serious threat to the Cuban people's freedom. Cuban rebels also needed American support. President William McKinley exerted tremendous pressure on Spain to free Cuba or grant limited self-rule to Cuba. Spain adamantly resisted. Then on Feb. 15, 1898, United States' battleship Maine mysteriously exploded in Havana harbor. The entire crew was lost in the tragedy. The United States retaliated by declaring War against Spain on April 21, 1898. The Spanish-American war resulted in heavy loss of life. American deaths were listed at 5,446. The War ended with the Treaty of Paris signed on Dec. 10, 1898. The United States had won freedom for Cuba.

William McKinley was elected president in 1896 and 1900. He won the war with Spain and guided America into world leadership. He was shot on Sept. 6, 1901, and died on Sept. 14, from the bullet wounds. Vice President Theodore Roosevelt succeeded McKinley. Roosevelt's progressive policies and determination to give workers and farmers "a square deal" made him very popular. He fought against business abuses by creating controls and reforms. He was a passionate conservationist. He placed more than 200 million acres of forest, mining, and water-power areas under government control. Roosevelt was well aware of America's obligations as world power. His astute leadership paid handsome dividends in resolving boundary dispute between Russia and Canada. The Panama Canal treaty led to the construction of a waterway between Atlantic and Pacific oceans. The 50.72 mile long Panama Canal shortened the distance to markets and saved businesses time and money. Roosevelt also protected South America from colonialists. His foreign policy was best described by the phrase, "Speak softly and carry a big stick."

Theodore Roosevelt picked William H. Taft as his successor for the presidency. Taft had a lower profile style of leadership. The progressive Republicans opposed Taft for a second term and supported Theodore Roosevelt. The once mighty Republican Party split and lost the election to Democrat Woodrow Wilson, who became the 28th president of the United States in 1912. William Howard Taft disliked politics. His interest was in the judiciary. Taft is the only president to serve as Chief Justice of the United States' Supreme Court.

Woodrow Wilson introduced legislation to keep businesses honest and workers happy. Farmers were provided with low cost loans and railroad workers were granted 8-hour work days. But while Wilson was busy with domestic agenda, Europe became engulfed in World War I. The slaying of Archduke Francis Ferdinand of Austria-Hungary triggered all-out war. Wilson struggled to keep United States neutral and to achieve a just peace. However repeated German sinking of American merchant ships led to a strong military response.

The United States declared war on Germany on April 6, 1917 and by

June 26; American troops were on French shores. About 2 million men in American uniform served in France. The tide began to turn in favor of the Allies as a result of American participation. The Allies captured and occupied several important enemy lines. The war finally ended on Nov. 11, 1918 when Germany signed the Armistice.

Even as war progressed, Woodrow Wilson was anxious to end the war and make peace. On Jan. 8, 1918, Wilson announced his famous Fourteen Points Peace Initiative. He envisioned the League of Nations as an international peace keeping organization. None of his peace proposals found support at home or abroad at the time, although he campaigned vigorously for his peace plan. His poor health and strong Republican opposition got the upper hand. On Sept. 25, 1919, an overworked, fatigued Wilson collapsed from nervous tension. He suffered a paralytic stroke on Oct. 3, 1919 and was confined to bed-rest. President Woodrow Wilson was awarded the Nobel Peace prize on Dec. 10, 1920 for his contribution to World Peace.

European nations suffered heavy loss of life as a result of World War I. More than 5 million civilians died of starvation, disease, and enemy or friendly fire. European cities also came under heavy bombardment and shelling. Homes, factories, schools, and transport systems were in ruins. Some towns and villages were completely wiped out!

Warren G. Harding was elected to succeed Woodrow Wilson in 1920. He advocated "Return to Normalcy." The nation was at peace. Harding embarked on a major speaking tour in June 1923 to revive confidence in his administration. He fell ill en route to San Francisco and died on August 2, 1923. The exact cause of his death is not known. Vice President Calvin Coolidge became the 30th president of the nation and continued Warren Harding's political agenda. During Coolidge's terms in office the United States made no commitment to enforce world peace.

The "feeling good roaring 20's" was a period during which the country as a whole prospered. There were problems such as political scandals, declining farmer income, and labor disputes. But people just felt light hearted after the war and went along with the "era of wonderful nonsense." During this period Henry Ford put the American middle class on wheels. People spent money for travel, vacation, resorts, and other fun events. At the same time many household appliances became available. Ready-made clothes, canned goods, and variety of everyday items appeared in the supermarkets. United States made impressive progress in education, science, religion, and literature.

Herbert Hoover was elected president in 1928. He promised to continue successful political agenda and popular economic policies instituted by President Calvin Coolidge. However within months of his inauguration the Congress yielded to pressure groups and passed the Smoot-Hawley Tariff Act. The law raised tariffs so steeply that many trading partner nations angrily reciprocated. The resulting impact on foreign trade was disastrous.

United States soon witnessed the worst business failures ever. The stock market crashed on Oct. 29, 1929. By the year's end, investors in stocks had lost an estimated 40 billion dollars! As a result of the market crash the country slipped into a most acute depression in its history. Every business was paralyzed. Banks and financial institutions failed. Factories and stores closed. Trains ran empty. By the end of 1930, more than six million Americans were unemployed and the number doubled within a year!

Herbert Hoover was soundly defeated by Franklin D. Roosevelt, who promised a "New Deal" for "the forgotten man." At his first inauguration in 1933, Roosevelt declared "That only thing we have to fear is fear itself."

President Roosevelt, true to his word wasted no time in dealing with

"The Great Depression" as it came to be known. The economy needed a massive boost. Reforms were needed to prevent future similar debacles. In a 99 day session upon the urging and direct guidance from the White House, Congress passed several important laws. One such bill created a Federal Emergency Relief Administration. This agency eventually spent over 3 billion dollars for direct relief for wages to millions of men and women working on public works projects. Another bill established the Civilian Conservation Corps (CCC) that employed men in forestry work, road building, and flood control. Other important innovative measures such as the regulation of the banking industry, Tennessee Valley Authority, Home Owner's Loan Corp, and Agricultural Adjustment Administration sailed through Congress to provide much needed relief, recovery, and reform. The Fair Labor Standards Act of 1938 set a minimum wage, a 40-hour work week, and overtime pays for hourly employees. It also severely restricted child labor.

Roosevelt introduced much important human welfare legislation as well. In 1935, Congress enacted several laws that authorized pensions to widows, the aged, the infirm, insurance to the unemployed, benefits to the blind, crippled children, and dependent mothers. Roosevelt gained immense popularity among the ordinary and not so ordinary citizens for his social welfare programs to combat poverty.

Like Woodrow Wilson, Roosevelt devoted much time and energy to domestic issues. Clearly, his presidential priorities were at home. He was neither keen nor interested in the conflict in Europe. However, aggression by the Axis alliance of Germany, Italy, and Japan escalated by the day. These countries were interested in territorial gains. Japan invaded Manchuria in 1931 and other provinces of China thereafter. Italy invaded Ethiopia in 1935. Germany occupied Rhineland in 1936, annexed Austria in 1938, and conquered Czechoslovakia in 1939. Continued aggression by Germany, Italy, and Japan provoked Britain and France. And then on Sept. 1, 1939, Hitler's forces attacked Poland. In retaliation Britain and France declared war on Germany on Sept. 3, 1939. Yet, the Roosevelt administration had no plans to be a party to the ongoing World War II.

Italy declared war on Britain and France on June 10, 1940. The Allies and Axis countries were busy at war and destruction. The Pearl Harbor surprise attack by Japan on Dec. 7, 1941, forced the United States Congress to declare war on Japan. A nation united, bursting with anger demanded punishment to the perpetrators of the devastating attack on the U.S. fleet at Pearl Harbor. Germany and Italy jointly declared war on the United States on Dec. 11, 1941. The United States reciprocated promptly.

The Allies won major battles in the all-out war. The countries comprising the Axis eventually surrendered one by one to the Allies. President Roosevelt was in poor health and died suddenly on April 12, 1945. Vice President Harry S. Truman was sworn in to be the 33rd President of the United States the same day. He had been Vice president for only 83 days! World War II had to be won. President Truman had his work cut out for him to say the least! But, Truman was up to the task. Germany surrendered on May 7, 1945. The Japanese refused to surrender. Truman, barely in office for less than a month made one of the most awesome, yet courageous decisions ever considered by one man! He ordered the newly developed atomic bombs be used against Japan. The first one was dropped on Hiroshima on August 6, and the second on Nagasaki August 9, 1945. War in the Pacific ended when the badly defeated Japan surrendered to the United States on Aug. 14, 1945.

World War II was the greatest conflict that mankind ever witnessed and engaged in. The war may have solved some issues but created many more. It caused major geographical and political changes in every country of the world. The magnitude of death and destruction was beyond comprehension. The actual cost of the war will never be known! The United States suffered heavy casualties as a result of World War II. Total U.S casualties were listed at 1,215,954! The U.S. death toll was 405,000 while 44,364 were listed as missing.

World War II expedited the birth of the United Nations. The main objective of this world-wide organization was to secure cooperation among all nations and ensure lasting peace for future generations.

Franklin D. Roosevelt was the only president elected four consecutive times to the nations' highest office. He guided the United States through its worst depression. Americans admired him for his skill and leadership and millions trusted him as a friend and a protector of the "forgotten man"! President Roosevelt also led the United States through its worst war; unfortunately he did not live to see the country triumph! He left a rich legacy that profoundly influenced the future of this country. The only super power and guardian of world order!

President Harry Truman proposed several progressive measures as part of his "Fair Deal." The Congress rejected many components of his fair deal, especially his initiatives for education and healthcare. The war-time U.S. industry quickly adapted to peace-time production. Television sets, electronics, frozen foods, and scores of other essential and luxury items flooded the supermarkets. Major industries such as electronics, chemicals, natural gas, jet aircraft, atomic energy, and many others expanded rapidly.

However the Cold War haunted Truman. It brought him troubles and success. While it established United States as the super power, the added global responsibility invited involvement in the Korean War. The Russian supported North Korean armies attacked South Korea on June 25, 1950. Truman rushed to support South Korean resistance. He ordered American troops to South Korea on June 30, 1950. The Chinese marched to war in support of North Korea on Oct. 25, 1950. Both sides suffered extensive loss of life. A truce was reached and fighting officially ended on July 27, 1953 along a line close to the original borders! The Korean War did not resolve any major issues but foiled the North's conquest of the South. American casualties for the Korean War were listed at 162,708, 54,246 dead, and the rest wounded or missing.

General Dwight D. Eisenhower was elected president with a big majority in 1952. Eisenhower had campaigned for change. Americans were not happy with the war in Korea. Eisenhower's promise to end the war gave him the advantage over his Democratic opponent.

The post-World War II era also hastened more Industrial growth. Automobile production accelerated. Many luxury appliances became available. Millions of new homes were built nationwide. The per capita income in the United States rose - so did the standard of living. The U.S. population increased from 131.7 million in 1940, to 179 million in 1960. The population gains were particularly impressive in the Western and Pacific states. Alaska and Hawaii joined the Union in 1959.

In the 1960's discontent was brewing among blacks, minorities and the unskilled labor force. Unemployment was on the rise due to automation of every aspect of industry. Slums and extreme poverty were visible in many major cities. John F. Kennedy, the newly elected youngest man ever to be president, promised progress and prosperity for all. His administration proposed far reaching civil rights legislation to help the poor and the minorities.

In October 1962, the Soviet Union under Premier Nikita Khrushchev, secretly established missile sites in Cuba. The missiles were capable of striking several U.S. cities. President Kennedy swiftly ordered the U.S. Naval blockade of Cuba. All ships delivering missiles and missile parts were ordered turned back. "The Cuban missile crisis" as its known brought the two super powers to the brink of war. The world breathed a sigh of relief when Mr. Nikita Khrushchev ordered all Soviet missiles removed from Cuban soil. President Kennedy had prevailed over Nikita Khrushchev! Kennedy was also instrumental in proposing and executing a treaty that banned all nuclear tests, except underground explosions. More than 100 countries signed the Nuclear Test Ban Treaty. America also put a man in orbit around the earth and Kennedy vowed to send man to the moon by 1970.

President Kennedy was assassinated on Nov. 22, 1963. Vice President Lyndon B. Johnson took the oath of office the same day. The 1960's were very difficult times for United States at home and abroad. On the home front, Johnson faced great discontent among blacks, youth, and a generally troubled nation. The War in Vietnam consumed his presidency. Johnson was a strong, skillful, and a persuasive politician. Johnson vigorously pursued and enacted Kennedy's ambitious Civil Rights Act through Congress. It provided penalties for discrimination in public education, government accommodations, and employment opportunities.

Johnson's landslide victory brought renewed energy and purpose to the new administration. The Great Society Programs stalled during Kennedy administration were enacted into law. The Economic Opportunities Act of 1964 endorsed a war on poverty. It provided funds to train unemployed youth, women, and minorities. The Act also provided funds for local projects to increase employment. Medicare for the elderly and Medicaid for the poor were introduced. Many social and educational projects were funded under The Great Society Programs.

Nationwide discontent, violence, crime, and social unrest became chronic problems for President Johnson. Every major city was in turmoil. Arson, looting, and riots were commonplace. The racial tension reached new heights when Rev. Martin Luther King Jr. was fatally shot on April 4, 1968. The tragedy provoked intense riots and civil unrest throughout the United States. A few months later Robert F. Kennedy, a presidential aspirant, was shot and killed on June 5, 1968. The country went totally numb. The antiwar movement gained momentum as a result. Americans were confused, divided, and angry over the widespread social unrest and the Vietnam War in particular.

Richard M. Nixon succeeded Johnson in a three way race to the White House. Nixon promised to end the Vietnam War and bring American troops home. As more troops died, the public unrest and dissatisfaction with Nixon's policies mounted. Demonstrations for peace were held in many major cities and on several college campuses all over the United States. On and off peace talks with the enemy continued and finally broke down in Dec. 1972. An angry Nixon ordered large scale bombardment of North Vietnam. This probably helped finalize the cease-fire agreement signed on Jan. 27, 1973 by all parties to the conflict. On March 29, an exchange of war prisoners was completed and the last of the U.S. troops departed Vietnam. The long unpopular war ended in March 1973.

The Vietnam War was the longest conflict in which the United States was ever engaged in. It drained American resources, patience, and caused heavy casualties. The American death toll from the Vietnam War was 56,263. More than 2,330 Americans were reported missing in action or captured by the North Vietnamese army.

Nixon's first term as president was remarkable. He faced many challenges at home and abroad. Inflation was on the rise, prices for essential commodities increased sharply. A Middle East oil embargo hurt Americans even more. Nixon was forced to devalue the dollar in 1972, and again in 1973 to cope with the nation's balance of payments.

President Nixon won high praise for his foreign policy initiatives. The U.S. lifted a 21 year ban on Chinese trade in 1971. Nixon visited China in Feb. 1972. He was the first American president to do so. He also visited the Soviet Union in May 1972. These visits led to many trade cum cultural agreements and improved bilateral relations. Perhaps the most shining moment of American history came when Apollo 11 Astronauts Neil Armstrong and Edwin Aldrin, Jr. set foot on the moon on July 20, 1969.

Yet Nixon is most remembered for the Watergate scandal that rocked his presidency. A failed burglary attempt of the Democratic Party Headquarters was directly linked to Nixon and his top aides. A series of missteps and distortions by Nixon and his associates further eroded public trust and support. Many of his top aides and associates were convicted for perjury and obstruction of justice. Congress was ready to impeach Nixon but he resigned the presidency on August 9, 1974. He was the only American president to resign from office. The earlier resignation of his Vice President also affected Nixon's presidency. Spiro T. Agnew had been forced to resign from office when faced with bribery charges.

To replace Agnew, Nixon had appointed Gerald Ford as his Vice President on Dec. 6, 1973. When Nixon resigned, Gerald Ford became the first President and Vice president in American history ever to occupy both offices without being elected! President Ford promptly pardoned Nixon on Sept. 8, 1974 for all federal crimes he might have committed while in office. Though Ford's move was widely criticized, many saw it as the beginning of a long overdue healing process for a nation that was so badly fractured and polarized.

Gerald Ford selected Nelson Rockefeller as his Vice president and retained all of President Nixon's cabinet officers. Ford's challenge was to restore public trust in government and elected officials. But the economy played spoil sport for Ford. He called it "Public Enemy Number 1." Record high unemployment hurt the economy even more. President

Ford announced several remedial measures to revive economic recovery but with little success.

Jimmy Carter defeated Gerald Ford to become the 39th president of the United States in 1976. Carter brought new ideas to Washington. The country was hungry for peace after many difficult, tortuous years of war. Carter quickly embarked upon a major initiative, pardoning all draft evaders and deserters during the Vietnam War. America's "healing" process had just begun.

President Carter stayed the course that Nixon charted in foreign policy. Carter worked to strengthen the ties between United States and China. He signed treaties with the Soviets to limit deployment of nuclear weapons. He devoted much time and energy to bring about peace between arch enemies, Egypt and Israel. The Camp David Peace Accord mediated by Carter was signed in 1979. Carter rightly won high praise for this accomplishment. The Panama Canal Treaties, signed in 1977, resolved another long standing dispute between Panama and the United States.

One of Carter's achievements was his unshaken resolve to provide leadership in areas of human rights and human dignity. He stubbornly resisted efforts by countries and leaders to indulge in human rights abuses. Carter used trade as a weapon by limiting exports to countries with poor human rights record and banned exports to those openly violating human rights.

Yet the Carter Administration is remembered for his economic failures. By 1978, inflation had become Carter's major problem. He announced several programs to fight inflation but high oil prices and market pressures pushed the rate of inflation to 13%!

President Carter's greatest challenge was the hostage crisis with Iran. In Feb. 1979, revolutionaries headed by religious leaders ousted the Shah of Iran. When the Shah was admitted to the United States for medical treatment, an angry mob supported by the new government took over the American Embassy in Tehran, and demanded the Shah's return. When Carter refused, they held most of the embassy staff as hostages in retaliation. Carter declined to negotiate with the Iranian leaders and authorized a rescue mission that ended in utter failure. The Shah died in July 1980 in Egypt, yet the hostages were not released until Jan. 20, 1981, Carter's last day in office.

President Carter lost his second bid to the White House by a wide margin to his Republican opponent Ronald Reagan. However Jimmy Carter continued to earn fame for his accomplishments as ex-president of the United States. He founded the Carter Center of Emory University in 1982. He also established the International Negotiation Network Council. Its primary function is to work and negotiate for peaceful solutions to conflicts among countries. His Atlanta Project provides help and support to destitute families. Carter received the Nobel Peace Prize in 2002 for his tireless efforts for world peace, the advancement of democracy, and human rights.

President Reagan's priority was the major economic crisis that he inherited from the Carter years. The record high inflation was hurting the main street and the wall-street! He proposed major legislation that included huge tax cuts to stimulate the economy. The proposal forced reduction in welfare and unemployment benefits. He also cut spending for several agencies of the federal government but sharply increased defense spending. As a result hundreds of companies applied for bankruptcy protection, the economic recovery stalled and the nation's deficit sky-rocketed! By 1982, the economy looked bleak while unemployment reached 10%! Reaganomics hurt the poor, unemployed, disabled, and disadvantaged. Reagan faced harsh criticism from the Democratic Party, women, and minorities. The economy improved slightly in 1983 and 1984, but the deficit reached record highs.

Reagan's foreign policy earned him much success. He was a gifted speaker and a great communicator. He developed friendship with world leaders that helped shape world events. In 1987, the United States and Soviet Union signed a treaty to eliminate all U.S. and Russian ground launched nuclear missiles with ranges of 310 to 3,420 miles. His foreign policy encouraged investment in the United States. During Reagan presidency people in general were optimistic and "felt good."

Like many of his predecessors, Reagan too had his share of scandals. He weathered the most damaging Iran-Contra affair. A Congressional committee blamed Reagan for failing to meet his constitutional obligation to "take care that the laws be faithfully executed." Several of his top aides were convicted of crimes while Reagan was still in office.

In 1988, George H. Bush easily defeated his Democrat rival Michael Dukakis to become the 41st president of the United States. Bush inherited tough tasks at home and difficulties abroad. The savings and loan industry was in a crisis. Over 1,000 failed Savings and Loan Institutions needed government assistance. The bailout cost the taxpayer billions of dollars. In Nov. 1990, Bush signed legislation to raise taxes in order to cut the nation's huge budget deficits. This was in direct contradiction to his 1988 campaign promise "No new taxes, read my lips." That broken promise cost him a second term in office.

President Bush enjoyed much success in foreign affairs. He won praise for his leadership and received international support when he sent American troops to intervene in Panama and Iraq.

The Persian Gulf crisis that led to war with Iraq was a unique situation that the United States and other countries of the world faced. Iraq invaded and occupied oil rich Kuwait on Aug. 2, 1990. On Nov. 29, 1990, the United Nation's Security Council demanded Iraq get out of Kuwait and authorized member nations to "use all necessary means" to expel Iraq from Kuwait if Iraq did not withdraw by Jan. 15, 1991. When

Iraq refused, Coalition forces led by the United States declared war on Iraq on Jan. 17, 1991. Bush ordered intensive aerial bombardment of Iraq and Kuwait. He also dispatched American troops to the region. The ground attack named Operation Desert Storm began on Feb. 24, 1991. Coalition forces entered Kuwait, soundly defeated Iraqi forces, and freed Kuwait. The operation Desert Storm was concluded on Feb. 28, 1991. Iraq was forced to destroy all weapons of mass destruction. It also agreed to a permanent ban on production of such weapons and allowed long term monitoring by the U.N. team of experts.

The Persian Gulf War of 1991 resulted in heavy loss of innocent lives during and after the war. Hundreds of civilians died due to lack of food and medicine. Hundreds of Kurds and Iraqi civilians opposed to Saddam's regime were killed in retaliation by Saddam Hussein's Republican Guards. Coalition forces suffered some casualties. Total U.S. death toll for the Gulf War of 1991, was 305.

President Bush enjoyed wide popular support and approval for his handling of the Gulf War. However a failing economy and the tax hike forced his defeat to Bill Clinton in 1992. Americans were concerned about the huge federal budget deficit, high unemployment, low productivity, and loss of manufacturing jobs. Additionally the public was restless over signs of growing racial tension, crime, and poverty.

President William Jefferson Clinton focused heavily on domestic issues such as the economy, healthcare, and welfare reform. During his eight years in the White House, Clinton paid special attention to the needs of minorities and women. He appointed more women and minority members to several top posts of federal government than had any previous president. He worked to improve the nation's economy by encouraging investments and tax incentives to small business and industry. Clinton was able to grow the economy, reduce unemployment, and even balance the budget. In fact the Clinton administration produced a $70 billion budget surplus by 1998!

One of Clinton's major achievements was NAFTA - the North American Free Trade Agreement. Congress approved the agreement in November 1993. NAFTA eliminated trade and tariff barriers to promote trade between Canada, Mexico, and the United States. President Clinton worked with the Republican Congress to encourage and increase trade with other nations through the General Agreement on Tariffs and Trade (GATT). This agreement signed in 1994, eliminated trade and tariff barriers among many trading partners of the United States.

President Clinton's foreign policy emphasized peacekeeping and nuclear disarmament more than the previous administrations. Clinton also faced tough challenges abroad just like most of his predecessors. He was able to arrest the flow of Cuban refugees to the American shores. Democracy was established in Haiti. The civil war that started in 1992 in Bosnia-Herzegovina was brought to an end in 1995, with a compromise that Clinton brokered. However Iraq remained a constant impediment to peace in the Middle East. When Iraqi forces attacked Kurds, Clinton ordered missile attacks on Iraq in 1996, and again in 1998. In March 1999, NATO forces led by the United States conducted heavy air strikes against Yugoslavia when that country attacked Kosovo. Clinton dispatched peace keepers to the war torn region and as a result a peace treaty was signed.

The Clinton presidency faced numerous political problems. Republicans controlled both houses of congress. The Congress initiated several inquiries into Clinton's personal life and financial dealings. His alleged sexual misconduct with Monica Lewinsky, an intern in the White House became a huge political scandal for Clinton. Based on Republican Kenneth Starr's final report, the House of Representatives impeached Clinton for perjury and obstruction of justice in Dec. 1998.

However the Senate found President Clinton not guilty of those charges in 1999.

The Clinton years brought prosperity to the United States. The strong economic gains were reminiscent of the 1960's! Unemployment was low so was crime. Americans were quite content with their newly found prosperity and the new direction the country was moving in.

Two term Texas governor George W. Bush was narrowly elected to succeed Bill Clinton to the White House. Al Gore, his opponent demanded a recount of ballots in certain Florida counties. George Bush and his brother Jebb Bush, governor of Florida were against the recount. The issue was later decided by the United States Supreme court in Bush's favor.

The 2000 presidential election was one of the closest and most controversial in the United States' history. Vice president Al Gore won the popular vote but Bush won the majority of the electoral votes!

The presidential race was extremely close in Florida, a state governed by Republican Jebb Bush. Earlier results had suggested a narrow win for Al Gore but as the vote count progressed, Gore's lead dwindled and George W. Bush was declared the winner. Al Gore requested a recount by hand in counties where the original count was in dispute. A frustrated Al Gore sought legal opinion from Florida courts. Gore's legal team argued that the machine count was flawed and a manual count was necessary to ensure that every vote was included in the final count. Governor Jebb Bush and Candidate George W. Bush were opposed to such a process. They argued that absence of standards for human judgment may cause even more confusion. The Bush v. Gore case was finally moved to the United States Supreme Court. On December 12, 2000, the Supreme Court ruled that the Florida vote recounts be halted. A 5-4 decision of the Supreme Court effectively assured a win for George W. Bush.

The George W. Bush presidency has mostly focused on fighting terrorism, wars in Afghanistan and Iraq. The terrorists attacked the World Trade Center, New York City's proud landmark on Sept. 11, 2001. Almost 3000 people perished in the fiery attack. President Bush ordered an attack on Afghanistan on Oct. 7, 2001. Several countries of NATO alliance also joined in the Military operation. Many of the perpetrators and supporters of terrorism were believed to be hiding in Afghanistan. Taliban rule of Afghanistan that provided safe haven to terrorists was also brought to an end. The Taliban is currently engaged in guerilla warfare against an elected Afghan government and the NATO Alliance led by the United States.

While allied forces were still engaged in Afghanistan, Bush ordered American troops into Iraq claiming that Saddam Hussein had stockpiles of weapons of mass destruction (WMD). On March 19, 2003, American and British troops invaded Iraq. Coalition forces captured Baghdad on April 9, 2003. The invasion forced Saddam Hussein from office and dictatorship. Bush declared "mission accomplished" and end of war on May 1, 2003. However hostilities continued due to insurgency. The coalition forces have suffered heavy loss of life. As of May 12, 2010, 4,401 U.S. soldiers have been killed and over 36,211 wounded. Other coalition casualties are not listed in this Guide. Iraqi military casualties are considered to be unusually high but the exact number cannot be verified. The Iraqi conflict has produced misery, death, and destruction to countless Iraqi citizens. Estimated Iraqi civilian casualties are over 1,300,000!

Team of experts from United States and United Nations conducted a thorough inspection for biological and chemical weapons (WMD) in all parts of Iraq - Bush's stated justification for war. No such weapons were discovered. However Bush has defended the invasion of Iraq arguing that the removal of Saddam Hussein was adequate reason. The unpopular wars of Afghanistan and Iraq, and continued occupation of those countries by American troops continues to haunt the Obama administration even to this day. As of May 12, 2010, the cost of these wars to American tax-payers has exceeded one 1.9 Trillion dollars and mounting!

The U.S. economy slowed in 2001 and has weakened substantially due to the 9/11 terrorist attack and its aftermath. The economy has further suffered during the second George W. Bush term. The adverse effects of sub-prime lending, mismanagement and several other factors have severely hampered the economic recovery leading to the current chaotic recession. The stimulus measures proposed by the Bush administration have had no favorable effect. Food and gas prices continued to soar as did the cost of living. Home foreclosures have escalated dramatically. Unemployment has reached all-time high in decades! Almost all economic indicators point to a long and painful road for economic recovery not only for the United States but for the world.

An extremely distraught nation elected Barack Obama as the 44th President of the United States. The voters heeded his call for change and the message to chart a new course to fix the economic turmoil of historic proportions. An eager, nervous nation is waiting for "the change we can believe in" as the slippery slope of global recession continues. Since his election, President Barack Obama has proposed a massive economic stimulus program to rescue failing banks and the automobile industry. Construction industry and other important sectors of the economy have also received much needed aid from the Obama Administration.

History Of Our Flag

The United States' flag is a symbol that represents the people, government, and our ideals. All nations of the world, rich and poor proudly display their national heritage and ideals through their flags. Citizens all over the world respectfully hoist and salute their national flags to celebrate national red-letter days, important national holidays, and festivities.

The U.S. flag, the pride of our nation, also known as the "Star-Spangled Banner" was made by Betsy Ross. It was officially adopted as the national flag on June 14, 1777. The flag is displayed all over America on federal, state, and public buildings. Americans also display the flag in private homes and front lawns with great pride.

The design of the United States' flag, also known as "The Stars and Stripes" or "Old Glory", was overhauled and changed several times. Samuel C. Reid (1783-1861) proposed a flag of 13 stripes, a stripe for each of the original 13 colonies, and a star for each state. Since 1960, "Old Glory" has displayed 13 stripes and 50 stars for the fifty states of the United States of America.

The colors of the flag have very special meaning. The three colors of the flag are reminders of: RED for courage, WHITE for truth, and BLUE for honor. Before public gatherings and meetings, Americans of all walks of life stand at attention, place their right hand over their hearts as the national anthem "The Star Spangled Banner" is sung or as they recite "The Pledge of Allegiance" to the flag.

The United States' Flag

Star-Spangled Banner

CHAPTER TWO
AMERICA THE BEAUTIFUL

The Land And Natural Resources

"Oh Beautiful, for spacious skies,
For amber waves of grain,
For purple Mountain Majesties,
Above Thy fruited plains,
America! America!
God Shed His Grace on thee,
And crowned thy good, with brotherhood,
From sea to shining sea"
Oh Beautiful, for patriots' dream,
That sees beyond the years,
Thine alabaster cities gleamed,
Undimmed by human tears,
America! America!
God Shed His Grace on thee,
And crowned thy good, with brotherhood,

From sea to shining sea"

Map Of United States Of America

Geographical Map of United States of America

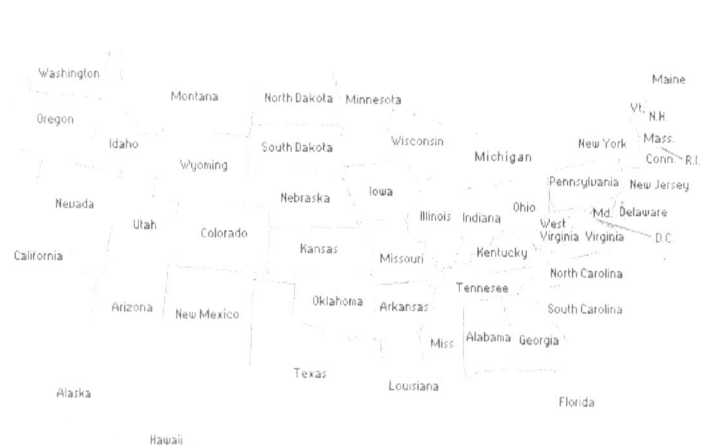

America The Beautiful is a popular and powerful patriotic song written by Katharine Lee Bates (1859-1929). American landscape, valleys, mountains, plains, rivers, and shorelines have unique breathtaking beauty: America is a nature lover's paradise. The song says it all! The melody to the moving song was composed by Samuel A. Ward.

The United States of America is the 4th largest country in the world. It consists of 50 states, the District of Columbia, and several outlying areas- the protective territories. The U.S. capital, Washington D.C. is located in the District of Columbia, state of Maryland. The United States, excluding Alaska and Hawaii is divided into seven regions. Each region is made up of states that have similar geography, climate, economy, traditions, and history. The regions are (1) New England States (2) The Middle Atlantic States (3) The Southern States (4) The Midwestern States (5) The Rocky Mountain States (6) The Southwestern States, and (7) The Pacific States.

In a vast and varied country like the United States, it is natural to have diverse climates. Some parts such as Alaska and the Northern regions are extremely cold especially during winter. Other parts of the country such as Florida, Texas, and the Southwest experience moderate to hot and humid temperatures most of the year. The country's highest mountain, Mount McKinley, elevation 20,322 ft. above sea level is located in Alaska. The lowest point, the Death Valley is 282 ft. below sea level is in California.

The land itself is vast, wild, and diverse. It has borders with Canada to the north, Mexico in the south, the Atlantic Ocean to the east, and Pacific Ocean to the west. The total land area of the country is 3,615,276 square miles. Excluding Alaska and Hawaii in the continental United States, the greatest distances are from east to west 2,807 miles and north to south 1,598 miles. America's pristine shorelines total more than 12,373 miles.

The land is divided into seven major topographical areas :(1) The Appalachian Highlands extend from the northern tip of Maine southward to Alabama. This rough region consists of several mountain ranges covered with thick forests and trees. It has vast valleys; some with fertile soil, abundant water, and large mineral deposits. (2) The Coastal Lowlands extend from southeastern Maine across the eastern and southern parts of the country to eastern Texas. This region consists of the Piedmont with slightly elevated rolling hills that separate the Blue Ridge Mountains from the Atlantic coastal plains. The Atlantic coastal plain extends eastward to the Atlantic Ocean. The Gulf coastal plain borders the Gulf of Mexico from Florida to southern Texas. Several rivers run through the Coastal Lowlands. The fertile soil and plentiful water supply has made the Coastal Lowlands a haven for agriculture. The rivers facilitate transport of cargo and raw materials for commerce and industry. (3) The Interior Plains stretch from the

Appalachian Highlands in the east to the Rocky Mountains in the west. These plains have many lakes, fertile soil, and vast green pastures for grazing. (4) The Ozark-Ouachita Highlands are located between the Interior Plains and Coastal Lowlands. Much of this region has poor soil for farming except for the land along the river valleys. This region has rich deposits of coal, petroleum, and metal ores. The Great Lakes and mighty Mississippi River provide water and vital transportation for agriculture and industry. (5) The Rocky Mountains are the largest group of mountains in North America. The mountains extend from northern Alaska through Canada and the western United States to northern New Mexico. Many rivers originate in the Rockies and flow to the Pacific Ocean. The Rockies have rich deposits of metal ores, minerals, oil, and natural gas. The Rocky Mountains' vast forests and timberlands support the building industry. (6) The Western Plateaus, Basins and Ranges are located to the west of the Rockies. This region extends from southern Washington State to the Mexican border. Part of this region is desert with little vegetation but there are some fertile areas where rivers provide water for irrigation. The Grand Canyon and Great Salt Lake are part of this region. (7) The Pacific Ranges and Lowlands stretch across western Washington, Oregon, and most of California with the Cascade Mountains to the north and the Sierra Nevada mountains to the south. Two of the Cascade Mountains, Lassen Peak in California, and Mount St. Helen in Washington State are active volcanoes. The Sierra Nevada Mountains consist of rich supply of granite. Many lakes and waterfalls originate in these mountainous regions. The fertile valleys west of the Cascades and Sierra Nevada mountains grow much of the nation's fruit and vegetables.

Most regions of United States have rich soil and generous water supply. This has helped United States to be the world leader in agriculture. Scientific advances, new technologies, and automation have also contributed heavily to increased farm and food production with reduced labor. About a third of the world's food exports originate in the United States. Wild animals, America's bountiful natural resource for food are still available. Beef cattle, dairy cattle, hogs, poultry, and other livestock are scientifically bred and reared in huge farms in the Midwest and the Southwest. Many varieties of fish are plentiful. The rivers, lakes, and oceans in and around United States support varieties of fish, shrimp, lobsters, and crabs. Some of the world's largest shrimp fisheries are located off the Atlantic and Gulf coasts. The Pacific coast provides abundant catches of salmon, tuna, and many more varieties of fish. American fishermen catch approximately 6 million tons of fish each year.

Travel in the United States is a breeze. The U.S. highways as well as the national, state, and county road systems are well planned and built for travelers' convenience. All parts of the country no matter how remote, are accessible via highways or paved, gravel, and dirt roads. Interstate maps and signs will guide you to your destination in the east, west, north, and south. East to west interstate highway routes have even numbers (I-80, I-90) and north to south odd numbers (I-71, I-75). The lowest numbered highways are in the southwest but the number goes up as you travel northeast.

Americans drive to work, shop, and for pleasure. Many households have multiple automobiles. The country has more than 75 automobiles for every 100 men, women, and children. The railway system in the United States was the primary mode of transport in the late 1800's and early 1900's. However with airline carriers crisscrossing American skies at convenient frequencies, people have opted for speed and leisure. At present, air traffic accounts for 18% of personal transportation, railways 1%, public transport, and personal automobiles improvise the rest. About 35% of the nation's cargo is transported by rail, 15% by trucks on interstate highways, and the remainder by ships and barges via waterways.

America is full of attractions - natural and manmade. Some regions of the United States have fascinating natural and manmade wonders. Every state of the union is known for something uniquely attractive and worth your visit! The ancient river gorges, water falls, national scenic highways, national parks, majestic mountains, thick forests, plains, pristine rugged shorelines, and much more are developed and modernized for visitor's convenience. Much information is available for you to choose attractions that interest you. Many places of interest provide room and board. Some places provide camping and lodging facilities for patrons. Maps, brochures, tourist guides, and books about any and all attractions are readily available from individual state Departments of Tourism, local Chambers of Commerce, Travel, and Information Centers, public libraries and book stores.

American cities, big and small offer many forms of entertainment. Most cities offer cultural, educational, and historical events throughout the year. Many cities offer seasonal sporting events such as baseball, basketball, football, ice hockey, and soccer. Most big and medium cities have museums of art, health, history, science, and technology. Your nearest botanical garden, theme park, zoo, and wildlife sanctuary may be just around the corner. All you need to do is inquire. Cosmopolitan cities such as New York, Chicago, Los Angeles, San Francisco, and many others offer much in the way of live concerts, entertainment, musicals, and plays. When visiting cities in the United States make it a point to inquire about the special events offered locally.

America's favorite pastime events are baseball, basketball, football, wrestling, ice hockey, auto, and horse racing. Of course there are other sports people enjoy too. Most sport fans buy season tickets to attend these events at a tremendous cost! Many patrons just walk in to the stadium or the sport arena to root for their favorite teams. In sports bars and homes all over the United States, people stay glued to their television or radio, watch every move, and miss no action! They wear their team's hat and jersey to support the team! They cheer, rant, rave, approve, and defend their team's every move and action with utmost passion, and with visible body language. That's what being a sports - fan is like in in the United States of America!

Most American families love outdoor activities. They know the camp-grounds, the lakes, picnic spots, play grounds, bike routes, and jogging tracks. They get all the family members involved for outdoor fun and games - the American way. Many communities, church groups, clubs, and organizations in the United States promote such seasonal events for charity or just for fun.

When you get acclimated to good old USA, you most probably will find yourself getting caught up in a life of leisure pursuits as most Americans do. Seasonal sport events such as football, basketball and baseball attract huge crowds and loyal fans. Friends and neighbors get together before and after the games for fun, refreshments, entertainment, and tailgate parties. Some families organize games and picnics. If you enjoy sports listed above and have interest in these events, be one of the fans. Invest your time and energy; get your family and friends involved for these activities. You will enjoy the excitement, company, and above all a neighborly phenomenon - a life full of fun in the United States of America.

Baseball Stadium

CHAPTER THREE
USA - THE LAND OF IMMIGRANTS

Language
The History Of Immigration To America
U.S. Citizenship
How Americans Live
Religion

The United States is the melting pot of the world. You will find people from all parts of the globe in major American cities, places of employment, and academia. United States is the most preferred destination to ambitious individuals, skilled professionals, students, and daring entrepreneurs. They are well aware that the United States has a long history of extending warm welcome to émigrés and visitors. Every year thousands of students come to pursue higher studies in the world famous American universities. Educators, engineers, physicians, scientists, and skilled technicians come to the United States in search of higher education, professional training, and employment opportunities. Then there is a steady flow of business people, visitors, and tourists. Almost all these immigrants have a common agenda - a better life for themselves and their families. A life with freedom to explore the possibilities, fulfill their ambitions, potentials, and above all their fondest dreams. Most of these immigrants quickly adapt to the new social environment. They observe, learn, and blend into one homogeneous society – the great American Society. Most of these new arrivals become quickly Americanized!

Americans have many things in common such as language, attire, food, and culture. Public education, hand in glove with mass communication, and the media have promoted a unique blend of American culture with a degree of common purpose and identity.

American society is an example and an experiment in multiple cultures and subcultures or cultural pluralism. This is evident in the pride people have in the land of their origin and ancestry. In cities and communities all over the United States you will find individuals and families from faraway lands living next to each other in perfect harmony. They are aware of the land of their origin and ethnicity! They follow their own traditions, speak their own language yet they coexist! But more than that - they have blended into one society. You will notice shops, restaurants, cultural events, parades, and ethnic festivals that obviously demonstrate the cultural diversity in the United States. The cultures cross and mingle in myriad ways to unite people in their adapted country - the new home! You will find Americans in general quite tolerant and inquisitive about new immigrants and most accommodating in any way possible, a welcome process for social integration.

Language

English is the most widely spoken language in the United States. All written and spoken communications are conducted in English.

All public business and personal correspondence is done in English. Banks, offices, courthouses, supermarkets, and shops conduct business in English. Almost all entertainment and mass communications are in English. Therefore it's imperative that you speak and understand English. It will be most difficult if not impossible to get ahead in a profession or find a good paying job without a good mastery of the English language in the United States. In recent years the Spanish speaking population has increased due to an influx of immigrants from South America. Many Americans speak Spanish language. Public and private schools offer Spanish language classes to students all over the United States. You will also often meet Americans who learn and speak other languages such as German, Italian, French, Russian, Japanese and Chinese. Given the current status of global influence on progressive American society, it will be safe to assume that there are several other languages spoken and taught in homes, schools, and universities in the United States.

Immigration To America

American natives, "the Indians" as referred to by the early European explorers were the first known inhabitants of this vast land for thousands of years. The Spaniards and the British arrived to America years after Christopher Columbus (1492) sailed across the Atlantic Ocean. Other Europeans arrived in search of wealth and opportunities soon after. The British were the first group of immigrants who crossed the Atlantic Ocean, landed on the east coast and established the first colony in 1607 in Jamestown, Virginia. The famous Plymouth colony, founded by the Pilgrims in Massachusetts was established in 1620.

The first wave of immigrants, mostly British, Irish, and Germans arrived soon after United States achieved independence. Tens of thousands of these immigrants fled to the "new world" to avoid political oppression, religious persecution, or revolution. Many of them came to explore employment and economic opportunities. Fewer than a million settlers entered the United States between 1790 and 1840. But by 1860 more than 4.3 million immigrants arrived for job opportunities in farming and manufacturing. Many who had been settled in the new world sent word to their family and friends in Europe about the opportunities and job prospects here in the United States. More than 7.5 million people emigrated from Europe to the United States by year 1870. The Irish mostly immigrated to escape from famine in their homeland. They had no money therefore settled wherever they entered the country. But the Germans had money to travel and move around the country. They were able to buy fertile farmland and settle farther away from their point of landing.

A second wave of immigrants from southern and eastern Europe arrived in the late 19th century. In 1907 alone the United States admitted 1,285,349 immigrants. And by 1920 a total of 23.5 million people arrived! Immigration to the United States from Europe continued at a brisk pace soon after World War I, and again after World War II. In 1921, Congress limited the number of immigrants entering the country with an annual quota system. The new system substantially reduced the number of new arrivals. The 1965 amendment to the Immigration and Nationality Act ended the quota system and replaced it with area wide annual limits on immigration. This amendment set a limit for new immigrants from the western hemisphere to 120,000 persons a year regardless of their national origin. The same law restricted immigration from the eastern hemisphere to 170,000 persons annually, with a limit of 20,000 from any one country. The 1965 amendment also brought a shift in the predominant sources of immigrants to the United States.

This was evident as large number of people arrived from Mexico, the West Indies and Asian countries in the early 1970's.

In 1978, Congress again amended the 1965 act by establishing a single annual world quota of 290,000 persons. In 1990, amendments to the Immigration and Nationality Act increased the number of immigrants allowed in the United States to 700,000 annually for 1992 – 1994 and 675,000 beginning 1995. At present the number of immigrants arriving from Europe has decreased. The largest groups of new arrivals to the United States are from Mexico, India, China, Vietnam, Philippines, Cuba, El Salvador, Haiti, Jamaica, South Korea, Bosnia-Herzegovina, and Canada. The United States' law has a quota exemption in order to provide humanitarian benefits for people who are persecuted on account of race, religion, political affiliation, and nationality. These immigrants are accorded Refugee Status or Asylum. People with special skills are also allowed entry to the United States under this provision. Hundreds of persons of this exempted category are admitted to the United States each year. But they too must prove their refugee status or the unique special skills they possess to the American authorities with credible documentation.

The Immigration and Naturalization Service (INS) was established in 1891 to administer and enforce immigration laws. The agency also determined the eligibility of immigrant aliens who wished to become permanent residents or citizens of United States. However after 9/11, this service and its functions were transferred to the Department of Homeland Security (DHS).

Some immigrants were brought to the United States against their will. For almost 300 years (1500-1800) European slave traders transported black Africans to the Western Hemisphere for sale. Some European settlers in the South owned large plantations on fertile farmland. They exported cash crops such as cotton, indigo, rice, sugarcane, and tobacco.

These mega plantations required large manual labor forces to cultivate and harvest crops. The farmers bought the African nationals - the slaves for forced labor. A slave was owned as his "master's property" and worked without pay. The owner provided food, clothing, and shelter for slaves.

Slavery was introduced in the United States in the early 1600's. It flourished in the South where farming on mega plantations was profitable. By 1860, there were about 3,954,000 slaves in the 15 southern states. President Lincoln's Emancipation Proclamation Act of 1863 abolished slavery in all Confederate States still in rebellion. The proclamation was a preamble to the 13th amendment to the U.S. Constitution. The states ratified 13th amendment in 1865 – the slavery was formally abolished in all parts of the United States as a result of Lincoln's historical proclamation. Former slaves were granted United States citizenship and civil rights after the civil war through 14th and 15th amendments to the U.S. Constitution.

Slaves performed a variety of important tasks such as cultivation, harvest, and transport of agricultural products. They worked as field hands. They planted, weeded, and harvested cotton, rice, sugarcane, and tobacco. House slaves worked as cooks and servants in the master's home. Most slaves worked long hours. The slave owner (master) had all the say in the matter! Some slaves became skilled craftsmen, carpenters, bricklayers, and riverboat pilots. Working and living conditions for slaves varied widely. Some owners routinely subjected slaves to inhumane punishment while a few rewarded them to extract more work. Hardly any laws restricted owners' treatment of slaves. Slaves lacked personal and legal rights. They could not marry a partner of their choice, own property, and earn their freedom. They were traded, sold, auctioned, raffled, or simply punished without warning at their owner's pleasure. Slaves often endured harsh brutality. Some slaves risked their lives to escape but very few succeeded. Slavery caused tremendous tension between owners and the slaves.

The Congress outlawed importation of slaves into the United States in 1807. The law took effect in 1808. The law may have stopped slave-trade in the United States but not the slavery! The Emancipation Proclamation Act in fact strengthened the Northern armies as thousands of slaves joined the Union Army and Navy. The Union Army also freed thousands of slaves during the Civil War. This action by the Union Army denied the slave-labor to southern farmers. The service and contribution of former slaves to the Union Army helped the North win the civil war! At present, the blacks in the United States enjoy legal rights accorded under the Constitution and are the 2nd largest minority group. Modern day America is full of highly successful, accomplished blacks. Many own homes, businesses, manufacturing plants, service and supply companies, restaurants, and entertainment companies. Employers in every sector of business and industry in the United States employ blacks for skilled and routine labor requirements. Blacks also work hand in glove with other citizens of the United States in other areas such as education, entertainment, and sports.

The black community in the United States is proactive and well organized. Martin Luther King Jr., championed equal rights and civil liberties for all Americans, especially blacks. The black community as a whole has made tremendous progress due to his nonviolent Civil Rights Movement. He staged sit-in demonstrations, campaigned to guarantee voting rights, and vehemently protested racial discrimination. He engaged the entire nation while demanding social, political, and economic equality for Negroes by peaceful means. As a result of his efforts, Congress enacted the Civil Rights Act of 1964 and the voting Rights Act of 1965. The high point of King's nonviolent movement was his famous speech "I have a dream that one day this nation will rise up and live out the true meaning of its creed: 'we hold these truths to be self-evident; that all men are created equal." The American black community is active in politics at local, state, and federal levels. Large cities such as Atlanta, Cincinnati, Detroit, Los Angeles, New York, and several others have elected popular black mayors. Americans have elected blacks to the United States' Congress, Senate, and Governorships. Thurgood Marshall (1908-1993), an illustrious jurist was the first black person appointed to serve as an associate justice of the U.S. Supreme Court in 1967 by President Lyndon B. Johnson. Thurgood Marshall served the Supreme Court with distinction until his retirement in 1991 due to ill health. The newly elected 44th president of the United States, Senator from Illinois, Barack Obama is yet another illustrious black political leader. He is the first black man ever to be elected president, a memorable historical first for the United States! His election to the highest office is proudly celebrated by the black community in the United States and by blacks elsewhere in the world. President Barack Obama is also cherished by most Americans as proof of America's commitment to democratic values and a fair electoral system.

United States Citizenship

Almost all of us are citizens of one country or another! Your nationality is usually dictated by and based on your place of birth and ancestry. Some may enjoy dual citizenship if the countries involved have such an arrangement. Naturally, all citizens have certain privileges, rights and responsibilities. These include but not limited to right to vote, the right to hold public office, and pay taxes. Most countries have laws to restrict or deny citizenship privileges to visitors and aliens. The United States constitution and laws passed by Congress give certain rights and privileges to visitors and immigrants. The law also sets guidelines and requirements to apply and receive permanent residency and citizenship of United States of America.

How Individuals May Qualify For U.S. Citizenship

- Through birth in the United States.
- By birth outside the United States to American citizen (s).
- By United States' citizen (s) adopting of a foreign under age child (not older than 18 years of age).
- By naturalization process. An alien may qualify to become a naturalized citizen by complying with the following conditions:

    A. You must be a legal resident of the U.S. for a minimum of five years.

    B. You must understand the rights and responsibilities of United States' citizenship.

    C. You must to be able to speak and understand English.

    D. You must take oath of loyalty to the United States. This also includes successfully passing a United States citizenship test. If you are an alien and wish to become a United States' citizen, make yourself familiar with the application procedures, citizenship requirements, and fees. Your under age children will automatically qualify for United States' citizenship along with you – all you need to do is provide required information.

- By matrimony: An alien or a foreign national is eligible for American citizenship if he/she marries a citizen of United States. However there is a waiting period of three years after the marriage for this privilege. Make yourself familiar with the procedures for application, citizenship test, and fees. It is advisable to engage an immigration attorney to guide you in this complex process.

How Americans Live

We intend to provide you some insight into how individuals and families live in the United States. In this Guide you will read much about the way Americans live in communities and neighborhoods. Quality of life is a priority for all Americans! Most Americans look for a good location and a fine community to reside and raise their family. Americans also care about good schools for their children, shopping convenience, safety, and many other amenities. Americans, more than any other people are on the move. Every year one of every five Americans changes his/her place of residence. Some do so for proximity to employment, convenience to church, and transport. Personal and family reasons are also a consideration to select new residence. The United States' economic system has a great influence on family life and choice of residential preference. Modern conveniences such as automobiles, dishwashers, and dryers, washing machines, frozen and ready to eat foods enable families to make time for leisure, recreation, hobbies, and other activities. Americans spend much of their free time at home usually watching television or working around the house. Hobbies such as dancing, gardening, handicrafts, knitting, music, photography, and other personal interests keep people busy throughout the year. Many families or groups that enjoy certain hobbies and activities attract like-minded people. They often promote their hobbies and special interests by establishing clubs for group activities. This form of social entertainment requires time, energy, and drive. Such kind of recreation brings much personal joy and satisfaction. As personal income is relatively high, people will pay to travel to cities and places of interest to promote their hobbies. They meet friends and make new ones! These interesting social activities are rewarding and also entertaining. The educational and recreational value of such an enriched life is all part and parcel of good life in the United States!

Neighborhoods, communities, and cities promote sport events, picnics, plays, musicals, and a variety of other activities for fun and entertainment. Many large and medium size cities maintain parks, zoos, museums, historical monuments, nature centers, amusement parks, water parks, and places of special attraction for the general public and tourists. Americans enjoy such activities and events throughout the year.

All large, medium, and even small cities in the United States have Chambers of Commerce that publishes informative guides for visitors and tourists. The general public, especially visitors and tourists can greatly benefit from such publications. For those who enjoy nature, travel, history, sports, or any form of recreation United States offers it all! Whenever you and your family plan a trip to a place of interest, history, and adventure be sure to request a visitor's guide and free publications from the offices of the city's Visitor's Bureau or Chamber of Commerce.

Americans are a law abiding people. The United States has Federal, State and Local laws. These laws make it possible for all citizens to live in peace and harmony. In order to pursue your dreams and goals in life, and to secure a bright future for you, your children and grandchildren these laws are absolutely necessary.

As you start your family life and profession in the United States, you will learn much about public and civil laws. While the public law regulates the relationships between individuals and the government, the criminal law regulates the relationships among people. One of the functions of this Guide is to inform you of the consequences of ignorance or negligence of the laws of the land in the United States. Always respect the law. The laws exist for your well-being and safety! As you walk/drive the streets, parks, visit the museums, nature centers, and other public places look for the posted signs such as "No parking any time", "Do not carry glass containers", "Alcoholic beverages not allowed", "Do not litter" etc., and by all means obey them! When in doubt about what you are doing or what is expected of you in such public places as described above, always get someone to guide you appropriately - preferably a security officer or a policeman. If none of the officers are available, ask a friend or a fellow visitor for help. You will certainly get the help you need and more! Play it safe rather than be sorry – the consequences of criminal behavior for you can be very severe.

Religion

There are scores of religions in the world. The major religions are Buddhism, Christianity, Confucianism, Hinduism, Islam, Judaism, Shinto and Taoism. Every society has a religion and there is no precise, simplistic definition for a religion. It's an organized system of beliefs (faith), rituals, and personal practices that embodies prayer and worship: all directed to a higher, supreme power or deity (God). And then there are people who are non-religious and atheists, who do not believe in a supreme power or a "Living God." Yet they too are good, responsible, and law abiding citizens.

The United States Constitution guarantees freedom of religion to all and does not dictate nor require that a person belong to any religious group or orientation. However the majority of Americans follow Christianity of the Protestant type. The largest Protestant groups are Baptists, Lutherans, and Methodists. The Roman Catholic Church in the United States has more members than any single Protestant group. Other religions such as Hindu, Islam, and Judaism have pronounced presence in many parts/cities of the United States. Any religious order or an affiliate can establish places of worship for the religious faithful in any region, state, and city in the United States. Several large and not so large American cities house Hindu temples, mosques, and synagogues for religious cum cultural functions and activities.

Your visit to a church or a place of worship may be a special event and a unique experience for you. Americans by and large respect you and your religion. They know that you promote your religion by praising God, inviting God's blessings upon you, your family, friends, and neighbors. I have attended many church services with my American friends and host families. The welcome I receive and joy I feel are beyond description! I have not encountered incidents during my entire stay in the United States where "conversion" was discussed or encouraged. Americans are acutely aware that religion is strictly personal.

CHAPTER FOUR
COMMUNICATION SKILLS

Greet People With A Smile
Verbal And Non-Verbal Communication
Body Language

Communication is an art of sharing information between individuals and through communication systems. We experience communication by means of hearing, seeing, feeling, and touching. Our mode of communication is achieved primarily by talking, singing, writing, drawing, dancing, gesturing, appropriate facial expressions, hand signals, and body postures. From the moment we climb out of bed until bedtime, we communicate routinely with family, friends, adversaries, neighbors, and coworkers. We receive and deliver messages by means of telephone, radio, television, and internet. Communications bring us breaking news from all over the world in a matter of seconds. The importance of communication and its impact on our daily lives, business, and industry can never be adequately stressed. Good communication skills are absolutely essential to define, express, and convey your feelings and strong convictions on matters dear to your heart. Your pleasant interactions, meaningful serious negotiations, and even mean-spirited bargaining require skill. As you strive to accomplish your goals, you will engage in much complex art of communication techniques. Your unique one of a kind outstanding winning approach, the gift of gab is what communication is all about! We would like you to think that good communication skill and success are inseparable. Truth be told, so is poor communication and failure! Therefore, first and foremost you will need to acquire effective communication skills, the key that will open doors to your horizons beyond your own expectations. The most important acquired skill that will guarantee your success regardless of your training, profession, and position is the gift, art, and method of communication. The message without an aggressive, seasoned, learned messenger is no message at all!

Language is the most common medium of communication. Verbal or oral communication consists of spoken words or speech. Singing is also considered a form of verbal communication! In contrast non-verbal communication is conveyed by facial expressions, hand gestures, eye movements, posture, and body language.

Greet People With A Smile

Whether in an elevator, hallway, classroom or common area pleasantly greet people you meet - those you know or even people you do not know. You may just greet them with "Hi, how are you? How's everything going?" or "Good morning", "Good evening" or other appropriate greeting. If someone greets you, respond cheerfully. "I am fine – and you?" or "I am well – how are you?" It's important that you reciprocate someone's greetings with affable cheer and friendship. Positive reciprocation to all greetings anytime anywhere brings out the best in both the initiator, and the reciprocator. At times these are the initial little steps one must take to build good, strong relationships. However adopt this approach and behavior to what is comfortable for you. Allow some flexibility and always know the context of the meeting for the appropriate greeting. Remember that greeting is acknowledging your friends, fellowmen, and acquaintances - it is meant to build and grow relationships with all you know, meet, and deal with.

Tips To Build Good Relationships:

- Always convey positive attitude towards others, be agreeable and constructive. Know that a relationship is a two way street.

- Treat everyone with respect. Try not to be critical. Look for ways to support, compliment, understand, and get along. Be honest and truthful.

- Your body language and personal demeanor must always project a positive self-image and chemistry.

- Whenever possible engage in activities such as sports, games, sightseeing, or whatever interests you and your friends/host/ guests. Learn to enjoy group and team events.

- Join clubs or groups that promote education, music, culture, and various intellectual cum social activities. You may also elect to become a member of sport team (s) of your interest.

- As you open door(s) to buildings, pay attention to people behind you and also in front of you! Hold the door open. If someone holds the door for you express your appreciation.

- When among groups and friends always be considerate to their needs. Give a helping hand if need be, hold automobile doors open, guide them to water fountains, or simply show everyone around you that you care about them.

- When among friends and acquaintances learn to share items such as interesting books, magazines, and even refreshments.
- There are occasions when someone may use a helping hand, by all means oblige if you can. If you receive help, advice, and the like always express thanks - a thank you note may also be appropriate.
- If your friends or neighbors approach you for favors and it's beyond your means or expertise, politely and tactfully explain. Do not accept tasks in which you lack skill or experience!

As you build good relations and make friends, your ability to understand and communicate with people, friends, and neighbors will become easier. Your life in the United States will also become more fun and enjoyable. Your friends and acquaintances make time for you, offer help to educate you, and also make you feel at home! Remember the learning curve never stops, accept all well-meaning help. Your social, intra-personal, and communication skills must carry the day for you. People around you appreciate and acknowledge your thoughtful, kind gestures and usually reciprocate.

Verbal Communication

The human development and language (speech) always go hand in hand. Linguistic abilities enabled mankind to eventually invent civilization and bring about technological miracles. There are over 6000 spoken languages worldwide, excluding dialects. The most widely spoken languages are English, Spanish, French, and Portuguese.

However there are more than 200 languages with a million or more speakers and 27 languages with more than 50 million or more speakers. Chinese is spoken by over a billion people and Hindi approximately 900 million. At the present time there is no universal language for global communication but English is the most preferred. English is the language of choice in the United States. Many Americans speak and write one or more foreign languages as well.

A great majority of Americans are familiar with immigrants from many lands. They understand and follow the unique accents with which immigrants speak. At times your American friends may ask you to repeat so they will know what exactly you are talking about. Cheerfully and patiently repeat what you said and explain in more detail if they still look puzzled. Most Americans speak slowly with an American accent. When you do not understand them, politely request an explanation. Thank them for their efforts and reciprocate when it's your turn. Americans pride themselves in dealing with idioms, current local vocabulary, and colloquial usage of terms and phrases. Their language mix is interesting and entertaining. Be well prepared to be occasionally "lost" but don't lose heart, kindly request a good lesson in idioms and the meaning of such idioms or phrases. Ask, "Will you please repeat or explain?" That will go a long way towards insuring mutual understanding and effective art of communication. Your communication skills will rapidly improve if you become an attentive listener. Practice listening to radio and television programs. But of course there is no better substitute than face to face, one on one dialogue. You will acquire good communication skills by a careful approach to learn and speak American English! As you develop and build better relationship with your friends and acquaintances your ability to communicate effectively will improve.

Tips To Improve Communication Skills:

- Pay uninterrupted attention to the speaker and wait until he/she is finished. Then ask your questions (if any), add comments, voice support, or dissent.

- Based on your own personal knowledge and needs address and approach each communication situation in a professional manner. If you are a student looking for advice meet with your counselor/teacher.

- If your teacher or supervisor speaks too fast or uses too much slang, too many idioms, phrases, and clichés make time to meet with him/her and explain your language barrier. He/she will make it easier for you.

- Join groups and organizations that promote spoken English. Some church groups, communities, schools, and universities organize classes and meetings for foreign students and visitors. If you are interested in advancing your English language proficiency, you should seize such opportunities to learn and improve.

- Learn the American accent by repeated exercises and tongue movements in private, preferably in front of a mirror. Radio and Television are a good resource to learn and understand skills of spoken English.

- Make it a habit to speak clearly and precisely so your listeners will understand. Get straight to the point and keep all communications interesting. Even your most loyal friends and attentive listeners may get turned off with a totally dull talk/presentation!

- Educate yourself by observing your American friends. Learn the customs, etiquettes, and social skills to deal with routine and professional interactions.

- Using a tape recorder listen to your tone and pitch. Decide which ones suit you and your personality.

- Practice speaking in various ways and learn to use your voice/speech pleasantly, interestingly, and forcefully.

- Make an effort to keep all communications positive, constructive, and neutral. Avoid subjects that are controversial but listen if no choice in the matter!

- Remember not to dispense opinions and advice to anyone unless such a request is made! Seek advice from trusted friends only if you MUST!

- Under no circumstances resort to foul, four letter words. Your well-meaning offers/requests will be denied and for sure rejected outright! Foul language has no place in professional and social discourse.

Non-Verbal Communication Skills - Body Language

Non-verbal communication is often as important if not more important than verbal communication. Body language is communication by means of arm movements, facial expressions, gestures, hand, and eye movements. Certain postures and body movements also qualify for silent signals! Body piercing, tattoos, hair, and clothing styles are a form of visible expressions indicating your tastes and dislikes. Your body language sends explicit message to the person (s) to whom you are speaking to of your identity, relationships, moods, motivations, attitudes, as well as your social and political views. Your pleasant non-verbal communication skills may attract individuals for a long-lasting friendship. Most likely this skill will also compliment your social, business, and personal life! The science of body language is known as "kinesics."

Facial expressions or gestures often send powerful messages of anger, happiness, and frustration more visibly than spoken words. At times some basic expressions of emotions such as sorrow, joy, and anger can be seen on your face much more readily than through words. Sometimes these expressions in some people may send mixed messages. The proper timely use of body language is a learned, cultural, social skill that can send strong and powerful signals to a person or an audience. The meaning of certain gestures and hand/eye movements may vary among different cultures. Certain learned expressions are also interpreted differently among different people. Body language may indicate your interest or lack thereof in a conversation or a particular situation. It's possible to send strong non-verbal signals to an audience, employees, co-workers, prospective employer, and an investor. Your cause will carry additional weight with proper body language and gestures that support your tone of voice and make your passion, motivation, and intent abundantly clear. It's been proven that facial expression, hand gestures, eye contact, and total body movements are true carriers of the substance, spirit, and force of your message. One of the proven ways to get the biggest bang for your buck in all dealings is to maintain eye contact with all persons you negotiate with. Eye contact will improve your negotiating skills, provide an advantage, enhance your position, and insure a clear edge over your opponents. The tone and pitch of your voice will show the passion and love you have for your cause and the unique position you hold. Sometimes your verbal advantage used with the wrong or erratic body language may antagonize and "turn off" your audience. You should pay special attention to synchronize your speech with your body language. While tasteful, appropriate body language and eye contact may be a powerful tool in any dialogue, inappropriate use of the above may spell sure disaster!

Body language may also help you discover a speaker in the act of hiding his/her true feelings. An astute observer will catch body language that does not synchronize with someone's spoken words. Usually when these do not match, listeners most likely believe the body language and non-verbal messages more readily than the person's spoken words!

Tips To Understanding And Improving Non-Verbal Skills:

- Practice certain facial expressions, hand gestures, and eye movements in private in front of a mirror. You be the judge.
- Have a friend or spouse help you with troublesome expressions and correct emphasis on catchy phrases.
- Synchronize tone and pitch of your voice with appropriate gesture(s), facial expressions, and eye movements.
- Practice speaking in various ways and learn to use your posture, facial expressions, eye movements, and gestures to convey messages tastefully, pleasantly, interestingly, and forcefully.
- Remember all non-verbal gestures and body movements must be in good taste.
- Overuse of body language may backfire so be cautious. Know your audience. Church groups, students, co-workers, friends, and neighbors may react differently to certain gestures.

Non-verbal communication certainly has definite limits. If you go overboard, the consequences may not be as pleasant as you like, and the results may even be disastrous. So adhere to tasteful body language and choice vocabulary to deliver your message at all times. That's when you communicate best and get the attention and respect you deserve!

CHAPTER FIVE
GOOD HYGIENE AND ATTIRE

Body Odor (BB)
Bad Breath (BB) - Halitosis
Hair Care
Proper Dress And Attire

American society in general is extremely health conscious. Every aspect of daily routine and social function is performed with emphasis on personal and public hygiene. Most American families keep their homes and surroundings clean, litter-free, and attractive. Children are routinely taught to take special care of their teeth, hair, personal health, and hygiene. Most adults pay careful attention to personal hygiene and physical appearance. You will also notice that most public places, parks, and streets in the United States are clean, attractive, and free of litter. Public urination, disposal of human waste, and dumping is not allowed in most open areas by law! You will also notice reminders posted as you walk the streets, parks, and public facilities – read the public notices and comply with the reminders in order to save yourself discomfort, inconvenience, money, and time. Public humiliation is not your cup of tea!

Body Odor (BO)

Sweating is a process by which the body cools itself. Most people sweat when the outdoor temperatures rise. Stress, fever, and fear may induce sweat in some individuals. Certain metabolic hormonal disorders and adverse health issues may produce profuse sweating. Sweat glands produce sweat and carry it to the skin surface where it is deposited. In some cases disorders of these glands may cause prickly heat. In some rare cases sweat glands produce excessive sweat (hyperhidrosis) or reduced sweat (hypohidrosis). There are two kinds of sweat glands: apocrine and ecrine. Apocrine glands are located in the groin and armpits. The rest of the body has ecrine glands. Apocrine glands secrete proteins and fats that enhance bacterial growth. The bacteria decompose the proteins and fats that produce body odor. Ingestion of foods and beverages such as curry, garlic, onion, and alcohol may also produce strong body odor. Sweat produced by ecrine glands is clear and odorless. However feet are an exception. We wear shoes to protect our feet, in the process feet endure a warm airless environment that promotes bacterial and fungal growth leading to foul odor. Certain inherited metabolic disorders that cause strong body odor require medical attention.

Body odor can be quite an embarrassing problem especially for new arrivals to the United States. You will most certainly experience rejection if you are in the process of just getting established in academia, the work place, and social circles. Body odor may also restrict and hinder the development of new friendships. Your friends may routinely avoid meeting with you! Usually as a matter of etiquette and good manners people may abstain from commenting on body odor, bad breath, and physical appearance. Most often than not they will go around you! Americans in particular readily compliment your looks, clothes, jewelry, shoes, and the like without hesitation! Therefore you must never assume that you do not and will not have personal hygiene problems. It is best to take steps to prevent such unpleasant episodes and completely avoid BB/BO problems. Prevention of bad breath and foul body odor is very essential to an individual's continued success and self-esteem. Bad breath may be managed by carefully selecting mouth fresheners, dental floss, and other products that work well for you. The most effective way to prevent body odor is to wash and bathe with scented soap daily and more often if necessary. After a good shower generously apply deodorant containing an antiperspirant. This will greatly reduce the rate of sweating and thus help control undesirable body odor.

As you get used to the American way of life, certain chores will come to mind. One such household chore is washing your dirty clothes. Make a point to get your laundry done as often as time permits. Clean clothes help fight body odor. Clean, nicely pressed clothing will give you attractive physical appearance, attract individuals, and gain favorable attention! Just a dash of perfume or cologne used sparingly can also be a big help. Too much perfume is considered inconsiderate. Perfumes can trigger allergies in some people. Be aware that strong scents may drive some people crazy!

Tips To Avoid Body Odor:

- Cleanliness is the key. Good hygiene is very important for your personal health. Daily showers with scented soap or shampoo are a must to maintain good health and avoid body odor.
- Be sure to apply deodorant containing antiperspirant

after shower. If you sweat excessively still, consult your physician.

- Scented creams and lotions are available in supermarkets and drug stores for men and women. Buy the suitable products and tastefully apply after shower. These creams also help fight your dry itchy skin especially during winter season.
- Wear socks and clothes made of natural absorbent material. Always wear clean clothes and undergarments. If need be, tastefully apply a dab of perfume or scented lotion.
- Wash your clothes regularly with an appropriate detergent and add fabric softeners to dry them well.
- Avoid foods that cause strong odors especially if you have a meeting or a social event planned. Make a habit to brush your teeth after meals. Use of mouth fresheners and mouth spray before meetings and public events is also very helpful.
- Avoid drinks that cause foul unwelcome body odor such as liquor, coffee, and the like before meetings.
- Maintain acceptable distance/airspace during meetings and conferences.
- If foul body odor is due to metabolic disorders consult your physician.

Bad Breath (BB) - Halitosis

If foul body odor (BO) is a turn off, bad breath sees no limit! People with infected throat, gums, and some rare disorders usually exhale bad breath. Once the infection is cured the bad breath goes away. Poor oral and dental hygiene is the main cause of halitosis. The inadequate care of teeth, gums, and soft tissues in your mouth may lead to infection of the gums and tonsils. Gingivitis or gum disease is the inflammation of the gums caused by plaque and bacteria around the base of your teeth. Bleeding gums, blisters in your mouth, and aching teeth need prompt medical attention. Some habits that cause bad breath are smoking, consuming alcoholic beverages, excessive consumption of coffee, garlic, onion, spices, and tobacco. Dry mouth (xerostomia) also produces bad breath in most people.

You can help control throat, gum, and soft tissue infections by periodic self-examination and regular dental checkups. Frequent use of appropriate oral antiseptics that kill bacteria also will prevent such infections. Professional care is critical in maintaining sound oral and dental hygiene and avoiding halitosis. Tobacco use in any form makes periodontal care and maintenance even more important, expensive, and difficult. Certain foods, varieties of fruits and vegetables increase saliva production in your mouth and fight bad breath. Apples, berries, cardamom, carrots, celery, citrus fruits, coriander, cranberries, melons, parsley, spearmint, and yogurt are some more products you may routinely consume to fight and avoid foul breath. The above mentioned products keep your mouth moist and may help fight bad breath to some degree - but remember it's no cure!

Steps To Avoid Halitosis:

- Thoroughly brush your teeth every morning, before bed, and after each meal.
- Regularly clean your tongue with a special brush or a gentle tongue scraper.
- Use scented, medicated dental floss after meals and before bed to clean between teeth.

- Regularly use oral antiseptics, mouth wash, and breath fresheners.
- Routinely consume fresh vegetables, berries, fruits, and above listed products that help keep your mouth moist.
- Avoid consumption of sweets that stick to your teeth and gums. Sweets encourage bacterial growth and halitosis.
- Avoid alcohol, tobacco, coffee, and such products before meetings, social events, and professional gatherings.
- If the above measures fail or prove inadequate, consult a professional. Regular visits to your dentist will help you maintain healthy gums, clean teeth and refreshing breath.

Hair Care

Body hair is made up of a protein called "keratin." Hair color is determined by the amount of pigment melanin present in the hair. Red melanin produces red and auburn colored hair. Black melanin is responsible for all other hair colors. In the absence of melanin, the hair appears white or blond. As boys and girls reach puberty, hair grows in the public and armpit areas. Boys also develop facial hair. Some women with Hirsutism may experience hair growth on the face and limbs.

Hair care is essential for your good physical appearance. You require professional help to manage and maintain your hair. Most men have their hair groomed and cut periodically. Most men prefer to shave and trim facial hair for a cleaner look and greater comfort. Most women take extremely good care of their hair length, color, and texture. Men generally do not shave their limbs. Women who are keenly aware of the appearance of their legs and forearms prefer to shave. Shaving is quick and safe but the hair soon grows back. Many women use depilatory creams for limb hair removal. Depilatories dissolve the hair just below the skin surface and help the skin feel smooth. Attention to hair color, style, and good grooming habits in men and women often invite deserved compliments. Job interviews, public events, meetings, and other social programs call for extra hair care. Your good looks will produce favorable results!

Hair Care Tips:

- Always maintain well-trimmed, tidy, clean hair. Men need to pay special attention to facial hair. It is a good habit to check the back of your neck, eyebrows, nostrils, and ear lobes. Attention to minor detail pays off!
- Women love to maintain and manage just the right length of hair, color, and texture. Most women maintain limbs free of hair. For that attractive, professional look frequently visit your hair care professional.
- Always look for the right hair care products in the supermarkets. All hair care products work but do not work the same way for everyone! Consult your hair care specialist for suggestions and desirable results that compliment your hair.
- If and when you consider a change of hair style and color, consult your beautician. He/she will be able to guide you appropriately.
- Remember "unruly" hair may invite unfavorable results. Let people judge you favorably - your looks matter a great deal!

Proper Dress And Attire

The weather picture in the United States is never the same everywhere. It varies in some places day to day! Climate extremes and variations are common in many parts of the United States – this is also true all over the world! Certain climate zones have unpredictable weather. While some places experience extreme heat, some may have warm comfortable pleasant weather, and some other areas may be freezing! It's very helpful to know about the climate/weather forecast of your destination in order to dress and protect yourself from extreme temperatures. You must dress appropriately to cope with heat, cold, and at the same time look your absolute best!

You must also know the place and occasion of your visit. Shopping, and family joy ride may not require careful selection of clothes. If you are invited to a meeting/function/picnic/program or a formal social event, you must carefully select your attire for the occasion. Most American hosts remind friends and guests what and what not to wear for the occasion. But it's also incumbent upon you to find that out on your own! Call your host or a close friend for suggestions and guidance. You do not want to be caught overdressed or under dressed ever; no matter what the occasion and the place! My own experience with over dressing to my colleague's birthday party turned out to be a huge disaster! For all occasions always wear clean clothes with a dab of perfume or cologne to feel at home and comfortable.

Helpful Tips On Dress Code:

- Know where you are going/invited to. Pick appropriate attire. Gatherings such as weddings, funerals, and professional conferences require clean formal attire. For job interviews and formal social events always select a freshly pressed dress, shirt, and suit. For informal parties, sporting events, and picnics wear clean clothes that make you feel at ease and comfortable.

- Know the outdoor conditions such as rain, snow, and heat. Daily newspaper, radio, television, and the Web will have reliable information under Weather. You may want to carry an umbrella, raincoat, and appropriate footwear if rain, snow or sleet is in the forecast.

- Know what the occasion demands. Tasteful selection of dress and footwear makes a positive impression. Places of worship, dinner/cocktail parties, and professional gatherings require formal dress and attractive footwear.

- Appropriate footwear for the occasion is a must. Certain events such as hiking, boating, and sports may call for special shoes and clothes.

- Certain informal functions such as picnics, sporting events, and family reunions call for attire that is unique or just fun. Some guests may dress as clowns, Uncle Sam or a celebrity! Surprise your guests - let that attire speak volumes about you!

- When invited to informal parties, picnics, and special events check your invitation! Your host may insist that you wear flip-flops, certain color of shirt, hat, and shoes for good extra fun - gracefully oblige.

- Never hesitate to show off your native costumes! You may dress for almost all occasions in your favorite native dress as long as it is in good taste. Americans love none better!

CHAPTER SIX
LIFE IN THE UNITED STATES

Visiting With Friends And Family
Inviting Friends And Families

There is no point in generalizing the way American society functions and individual families live. Most American families have their routine. They keep extremely busy and occupied with chores in and around the house throughout the year! Families with school age children may have additional obligations such as driving their children to and back from school and help with home-work! Some parents have to take their children to Childcare Centers before reporting to work. The families make these arrangements well in advance with plan A and plan B! Most families plan their vacation, picnics, parties, family reunions, and other activities months in advance. A good plan always begets good results! This is how families function in American cities and suburbs. If you visit the countryside and rural areas of the United States, you will find quite a different kind of routine. No hustle, slow pace, and sort of laid back attitude! Most visitors and newcomers choose to live in and around urban or suburban areas in the United States - this Guide mostly deals with such living.

Visiting With Friends And Family

Americans in general are a fun loving people. They enjoy the great outdoors, cookouts, and picnics. When outdoor recreation is not planned, they can be found dining in restaurants, entertaining guests or engage in activities in and around the house. Americans love diversity. Many American families enjoy entertaining foreigners like you! Your native tongue, culture, and unique customs will immensely intrigue them so be prepared to be invited to share.

I arrived in Cincinnati on a pleasant sunny day in September. I started my very first job the very next week. I met a lovely couple the following week at work. Barely able to speak and understand (American) English, I was able to convey my reasons for being in the United States. Even so I was invited to their beautiful country home in Kentucky that weekend. There was a large gathering, an interesting mix of people-- business owners, physicians, teachers, and family members. My dear hosts made time and effort to introduce us (my brother and myself) to all present. Everyone was friendly. Dr. T. Roberts, an eminent Geologist, who had been to India on many occasions, treated all of us to a Geology lecture and slide show about India!

We had a great dinner. The hostess, Mrs. Fullerton gingerly cooked classic American dishes such as ham, fried chicken, salads, and vegetables. There were favorite deserts such as apple pie, lemon merengue pie, peach cobbler, and varieties of ice cream. When I accepted the invitation little did I know that I was the guest of honor and my host family's intent was to treat me for a taste of America – food and people! For the next

35 years I had the distinct pleasure of visiting "my Kentucky home" for every important and even some not-so-important occasions.

I have had the good fortune of meeting dozens of American families like the Fullerton's. The co-author of this Guide, Kenneth Brand and his gracious wife Marilyn, routinely entertained foreign students and families. Occasions such as Independence Day (4th of July), Thanksgiving, Christmas, and Easter are celebrated with extravagance with special friends and families in the United States. I mention these personal experiences to inform you of the kinds of friendly reception that await you in this great country.

When invited to an event such as picnic, Thanksgiving dinner, Christmas family gathering, New Year's party, birthday, anniversary, wedding, or just a weekend get-together make it a point to go. Remember to dress appropriately, wrap an appropriate gift for that occasion, and be at the venue on time. The hosts will welcome you at the door and introduce you to everyone present. Greet them all and make yourself at home. Enjoy the time, company, and food. Take interest in what everyone does such as games, sports, music, conversation, and other planned activities.

Most Americans will actively participate in every aspect of the event such as distributing drinks, passing around snacks, and if need be setting up tables with plates, cups, chairs, and utensils. You will notice many guests cleaning and doing dishes -- so don't hold back. Join the fun - I did! I greatly enjoyed helping my hosts before and after the parties. I knew that my contribution was appreciated. As you take leave for the day/evening, thank your host for a memorable time and at your earliest convenience drop them a "Thank You" note to tell them how much you enjoyed the evening, company, conversation, and the atmosphere. You may also point out something that made your visit special and memorable --- that's the American way!

Many American families "adopt" foreign students and families. If you are invited to such an arrangement, gladly entertain the offer. Being adopted by a hosting American family is a huge advantage to you and to them. It's a learning experience for the host and the adopted party. While you learn American ways, their customs and culture, the host family will enjoy learning about your culture, customs, and much about your distant homeland. Be sure to tell your host about you and your ambitious plans. This sharing will benefit you immensely. Many host families love to take greater interest in foreign students, professionals, and families in order to properly guide them in the United States. So make sure to avail yourself of the opportunity of a life time. I have had the pleasure of being adopted by the Fullerton family and then by the Gambino family while in school. Besides the Fullertons and Gambinos, I had the pleasure of being a frequent house guest and a friendly visitor with Blinzlers, Brands, Christofels, Greens, Hiltenbeitels, Musekamps, Nartkars, and Rincks to mention a few! I received plenty of good advice, guidance, and valuable support from all these kind, caring families. I still visit many of these supportive families and friends for fun and friendship. We invite them over to our house for special occasions such as birthdays, anniversaries, or just for fun times! It pays to nurture the relationship and maintain the friendship. The emotional support, the joy of exchanging periodic visits, and the indigenous advice you will receive are truly priceless! You are certain to walk into situations like I did within a short time upon your arrival – so be prepared!

Some American families enjoy close relationships with families from other countries as well. Entertain such an arrangement if you have your family with you. The social and cultural barriers are much easier to overcome when trust and friendships grow. Such relationships will bring much joy and great mutual benefits to the families involved. This arrangement may immensely benefit children of both parties.

Most universities and colleges in the United States also take great interest in foreign students and families. The International Student Organization, the Campus International Student Center, and Foreign Student Advisors often plan and organize year round activities for foreign students and families. These events are planned for your benefit. Americans understand that foreigners have special needs such as companionship, guidance, and a helping hand! You will run into many interested families and individuals with good intentions. Make time to meet and greet them all! Explore and find people with interests similar to yours. Befriend them for long term or just casual interactions - you will be glad you did!

For events such as above always check the school bulletin board, school newspaper or simply keep ears to the ground. The local visitor's bureau, daily newspaper, radio, television, and public library may also provide useful information about events off campus.

Useful Tips To Enjoy Your Social Activities:

- When invited for occasions such as birthdays, 1st communions, and receptions be sure to be on time. If the party is for adults only leave your kids with a baby sitter.
- If children are allowed, by all means take them along but remember to keep an eye on them at all times. Well behaved kids always bring pride and joy to parents.
- If you have a friend you would like to bring to the event, let the hosts know ahead. Offer to bring a dish or desert from your native land, your host may welcome it. The dish must not be a substitute for a planned gift for the occasion no matter what the occasion is.
- Parties and social events usually offer food and drinks. It's

a good habit to eat and drink in moderation. Know your limits.

- Make a point NOT to be the first in line for food and drinks. Be patient and pleasant, your turn will come. Serve yourself small portions, enjoy your favorites, and go back for more - only if plenty of food is available. Be considerate of all present at the gathering.
- If you are not quite sure how to use utensils such as knife, fork, and spoon request a quick demonstration from a friend. He/she will certainly oblige.
- Chew and swallow food and beverages with minimum noise. It is bad manners to "slurp or burp" during or after meals.
- Make it a point to speak English with everyone including your spouse and compatriots. Speaking your native tongue may offend guests.
- Abstain from discussing controversial subjects such as politics, race, and religion. These are very personal matters and are not usually subjects for social gatherings.
- Always engage in pleasant discussion of non-controversial neutral subjects such as sports, music, science, literature, art, history, geography, and current world events!
- Never discuss family issues nor try to resolve disputes among friends. Your guests will not entertain nor approve such behavior.
- Always offer to help. Whatever you can do to make work light for the hosts will be most welcome!
- You may also offer to entertain your hosts if you are able to perform acts such as dance, music, and the like - all will enjoy your efforts.

- If for reasons you are unable to attend the party, call your host at your earliest to inform. Doing so at the last minute is inconsiderate.
- Always make time to mail a friendly "Thank You" note to your host at your earliest convenience. You may want to point out what made your visit so memorable and entertaining.

Inviting Friends And Families

It is fun to invite friends and families to your house if you are able to entertain. Invite them at your convenience and treat them with your country's favorite dishes. They will enjoy such an experience. When planning a party for an occasion, develop a list of guests, double check the list. You must inform/invite your guests at least 2-4 weeks in advance. Your guests will most gladly join the party for fun, food, and recreation. As much as possible arrange for a demonstration of your hometown favorites such as traditional music, customs, food, and beverages. If it's a wedding ceremony, adhere to your native customs! Americans love witnessing traditional ceremonies and customs from distant lands. There are no guidelines to being a good host. Just use your best judgment, greet and acknowledge everyone at the door, and definitely let them loose. It's appropriate to inform your guests about the food, the duration of the party, the dress code, and the like. If you are serving foods and beverages from your native land, take a minute to introduce the dishes to your guests. Let them know what is in it - such as very hot spices and the kind of filling or meat (poultry, pork, lamb, fish, and vegetarian). The guests will truly appreciate your descriptions and your consideration - more reasons to sink their teeth into your delicious food!

Some Useful Party Tips:

- If your party is outdoors inform guests to dress accordingly.
- If swimming is planned for the party be sure to have enough towels and other bathing accessories.
- Inform your guests of the kind of food you plan to serve. Prior dinner time, take a minute to educate guests on all native foods, specialties, and drinks. Remember all cooked foods may look alike to your novice guests. Point out the vegetarian and non-vegetarian dishes.
- Most Americans love to serve themselves – all you need to do is arrange, decorate, set up tables, chairs, utensils, and the varieties of food and drinks.
- Some guests may be expecting prayer before dinner -- please oblige.
- It is quite appropriate to plan a program. You may choose to entertain your guests with dance, games, movies, music or any other tasteful cultural activity for the occasion.
- Most American guests will bring an appropriate gift for the occasion. Remember to open gifts before they depart and thank them as you open the gift(s). Always mail a "Thank You" note at your earliest convenience reminding them how thoughtful they were to share the occasion with you.
- Provide a map or directions to your residence. Your guests will definitely appreciate your thoughtfulness.
- It's also appropriate to put out balloons at the entrance gate to your residence – a very visible inviting sign!

As you get your feet wet in the United States you will eventually adapt to American way of living! One of the favorite family events I enjoyed throughout my stay in this country is dining out. All of us dress up, put on our best behavior, and visit our favorite restaurant for brunch or dinner. We follow the simple rule - we order our favorite dishes and enjoy what we order! It's a great treat for everyone and good fun for all. Occasionally we invite our American friends and families for brunch or dinner. In return those families do the honors for us – the American way! We also enjoy other activities such as picnics, baseball, football, and soccer. When involved in such group and family activities make sure that you share all expenses equally with all participants. And for added fun here are some friendly suggestions.

- Always be punctual for such group activities. It's nice to be at the venue ahead in order to get ready and organized.
- Be a part of the whole project/event. Engage yourself with whatever you can do to make the event a success!
- If the group is meeting in a restaurant dress tastefully and be on your best behavior. Whistling, abusive tone and language to receive service may not go well with your group members. Be polite and respectful to servers, waiters and the restaurant staff!
- When the party is over and it's time to pay make sure that you are just as generous as the rest of the group – contribute your share including a very generous gratuity (tip) to your server.
- If the gathering is outdoors, get involved in every aspect of the party such as setting tables, chairs, utensils, drinks, and food.
- If games are planned get into the act. There is always something you can contribute!
- When it's time to call it quits, check with everyone - offer

whatever help you can. Be a nice person - earn those extra credits!

Entertaining guests is one of the safest and best ways to make friends and eventually develop lasting relations. Not only you meet existing friends often, you will also make more friends as you visit and invite new families for fun and recreation. It's also an occasion to share and enjoy social and cultural activities in the United States. As you get involved in social and community affairs, you come across many opportunities to learn and understand American way of life and above all the great American spirit of caring and sharing. As a well-informed visitor, you will be better equipped to create and promote your own sense of family priorities and community obligations. All you need to do is try!

CHAPTER SEVEN
STUDENT LIFE IN AMERICA

The Admission Process To The School Of Your Choice

Your Resume

The system of education in United States is much flexible, innovative, and progressive. The federal and state administrations plan and finance education and job-training for all. Like many countries, the U.S. does not have a national educational system. Each state in the United States is responsible for developing, organizing, promoting, and regulating its own system of education. The systems developed by states have much in common. This is an advantage to prospective students when selecting a college or university. The students have unlimited freedom of choice! The United States Department of Education finances and administers several programs to promote and improve educational excellence nationwide. The goal is to provide equal educational opportunities to all children.

The educational system in the United States is more geared to application to what you study in the classroom. The American system is also flexible and easily adaptable. This flexibility has encouraged educators and teachers to develop and introduce latest teaching techniques in the classroom. With modern text books and advanced curriculum the entire process seems to deal with current events! Whether you major in arts, science, or any other special subject, you are taught current events, trends, and developments along with required basics. Most foreign students require a few months to understand and master the system of education in the United States. Most colleges and universities in the United States follow the calendar or the program of a school year as described below.

- Semester system: The school calendar is divided into two semesters of about 16 weeks each. The first semester begins in late August or early September. The second semester begins in mid-January or early February. The school calendar year ends in May or early June with commencement or graduation gala!

- The quarter system: The school calendar is divided into four quarters of 10, 11, or 12 weeks each. The first quarter (fall quarter) begins in September. The second quarter (winter quarter) begins in January followed by the third quarter (spring quarter) that begins in late March or early April. The final summer quarter is offered in June but many students opt out of this quarter for various reasons.

- The trimester system: The school year is divided into three trimesters of about 15 weeks each.

Educational institutions have guidelines and rigid requirements for students in selecting their courses. Almost all colleges and universities have certain required subjects and some optional (elective) subjects.

The freshmen class is expected to register for introductory subjects. Sophomores, juniors, and seniors enroll for advanced subjects in their declared major field of study. Whether the school is on a semester or quarter system, a student must complete a required number of credit hours to graduate with a degree or diploma.

Student life in the United States usually starts with much fanfare. Before classes actually begin in the fall, all freshmen are required to attend an orientation program sponsored by the school. The program includes a tour of the entire campus and dormitories. Students will visit places such as the cafeteria, classrooms, gymnasium, library, laboratories, and computer center. You will also visit The Admissions office, Dean's office, and Registrar's office. The orientation program is attended by almost all freshmen and their parents or guardians. Student life on the campus becomes easy when you know your way around!

Your college or university will assign a counselor to guide and assist you while in school. Your counselor will introduce you to the college faculty, administration, and other school officials if requested. If you need help and advice in your studies, language, job search, and any other reasonable necessity, always make an appointment with your counselor or teacher. Explain your situation calmly and clearly. If you are bit nervous, write your requests in the order of priorities and tactfully seek solutions and advice so you may receive the right kind of help!

College life away from home gives students a good measure of freedom and independence. It also places a degree of discipline and responsibility! Student life in the United States is full of social activities, multiple assignments, homework, term papers, and individual or group projects. A student living on the campus has obligations such as shopping, house chores, cleaning, and laundry. Social life and campus activities are also part of student life! The initial quarter or semester may be a bit imposing but as you get your feet wet, budget your time and get organized, you will see the light at the end of the tunnel!

Each year millions of college and university bound students rack their brains to secure a seat in the school of their choice. The process is a Herculean challenge! The process itself must start with careful search of schools that offer academic or athletic programs that you intend to pursue! It involves interviews, meetings with student counselors, and also meetings with alumni of the prospective college or university. You must always consult your high school academic advisor before you eliminate schools and select the one that fits well with most of your requirements. You must consider factors such as academic program, athletic program, staff, class size, availability of scholarship, and total cost of your education. Education beyond high school prepares young men and women for professions such as doctors, engineers, lawyers, and teachers. Therefore prospective students must choose the school that most nearly fits their needs and desires. Your professional excellence is also judged by the college or university that you attend!

Foreign students seeking admission to colleges and universities are required to have their credentials evaluated by recognized professional evaluating agencies. This process must be completed before admission is granted to a college or university of your choice! Your school will recommend an evaluating agency that they trust and rely upon in order to place you in a cohesive academic group. Your evaluation results are reported directly to the college or university. This process facilitates your academic counselor to guide you properly. You may enroll in the appropriate courses of study and choose introductory or advanced subjects in your field of interest. This is a tremendous benefit to students arriving from countries where the standard of education is not on par with that of the United States' standards. The evaluating agency will develop your academic profile based on your grades, years of study, and the curriculum. The agency may even point out your educational strength, deficiencies, and recommend remedies to you.

Tips To Prepare Yourself For Admission To The School of Your Choice:

- Know what your interests are and what program (s) you want to pursue.
- Develop and document your vision and your academic goals.
- Develop a short list of colleges or universities you wish to attend. The Schools on your short list must offer courses of your interest! The schools must have adequate facilities, amenities, and proper accreditation. Class size, quality of staff, and teaching methods are also important considerations!
- Meet with your current student counselor or academic advisor as needed for guidance. Your counselor will help explore the availabilities of scholarships, student loan or aid, and other benefits. He or she may also help you prepare for entrance exams and other competitive requirements if requested.
- It is appropriate and highly recommended that you meet with representatives and alumni of school (s) on your short list. Most foreign students are not able to meet college or university representatives therefore they must devise ways to circumvent this handicap with serious extra efforts.
- You must make time to visit all the schools you plan to apply. Take a guided tour of the campus. Visit the gym, library, student center, admissions office, and Dean's office. Know

your way around the campus. Also walk/drive outside the campus – know the streets and neighborhood!

- You must know that most colleges and universities compete for students with exceptional abilities. Showcase your unique talents in academia or athletics and be a much sought after standout applicant.

- As you receive admission to multiple schools, you owe it to yourself to choose the one that fits best for you! Your academic/athletic goals should be your priority.

- A successful school search must also include understanding of campus and dormitory living, cost containment, and budget restraints. We recommend that you refer to some of the publications available in your local and college library. The publications also contain information on financing your entire education. For your benefit and convenience we have listed a few such publications below.

1. Fiske Guide to Colleges.
2. The Princeton Review – Complete Book of Colleges.
3. U.S. News & World Report – America's Best Colleges. U.S. News & World Report - America's Best Graduate Schools.
4. Peterson's Guide to College Visits. (2002).
5. The Insider's Guide to the Colleges- Compiled and Edited by The Staff of The Yale Daily News (2008), 34th Edition.
6. 100 Ways to Cut the High Cost of Attending College - By Michael Viollt.
7. Funding Education Beyond High School – The Guide to Federal Student Aid. 2008-09. U.S. Department of Education Federal Student Aid.

Once you have selected your college or university, it's wise to make time to do some serious reading! Read publications such as Peterson's

Guide to College Visits, a college survival guide, campus life, living on the campus, and the dormitory life. As a student looking to excel in academics or athletics, refer to these resource guides for tips on how to adapt to living on college campus. A well prepared student has success written all over him/her! The choice is yours. Modern education is a true challenge but you can excel if you follow some innovative ideas of your own!

Many American educational institutions are affiliated with foreign colleges and universities. Part of your studies may be offered in these foreign schools. If you are interested in this kind of arrangement, make sure you seek and understand the process well. Know the Passport/Visa requirements, approximate cost of tuition, living expenses in the selected country and the school you will be earning your partial credits. You must also know the duration of your stay in the selected country and school. Remember that your safety and security are also important considerations. Your library has resources available to prepare you for this exciting experience. Look for student guides to study abroad and the country/school of your choice. Learn the country's culture, customs, geography, and history. Make yourself familiar with your host country's language and educational system before you enroll in the program.

Most college and high school students in the United States budget their time in order to carry on full or part time employment based on their financial needs. Then jobs may pay part of their tuition and living expenses. Some students earn money to support expenditures for an automobile, personal necessities, and social life. A vast number of students also opt for student loans that are repaid after graduation. However foreign students may not qualify to receive student loans. The following restrictions apply to most foreign students.

- You may not seek job opportunities outside the college campus.

- You may not qualify for student loans, grants, and other benefits.

Foreign students must have enormous patience and good social skills to succeed in the United States. This Guide is designed for you to discover and sense some of the hurdles you will face as a student. Always plan ahead, budget your time to accomplish your studies, interests, homework, household chores, and social obligations. The American educational system is geared towards attention to detail and your application of what you have learned in the classroom. A student must know the educational system in order to excel in it. Teachers take pains to create a relaxed, pleasant classroom atmosphere that is conducive to learning for all. If you encounter serious hardships and it's difficult for you to continue your education, do not let studies suffer, rather, seek guidance from your academic counselor, your teacher, and possibly even your Foreign Student Advisor. In some instances your teacher and advisor may even recommend personalized solutions to your unique situation so your studies will proceed as planned. At times you may encounter serious financial shortfall. This is one of most serious problems many foreign students frequently face due to the high cost of living in the United States. Meet with your counselor, teacher, and the Foreign Student Advisor by appointment! Explain your difficulties in a calm, composed manner - you may get the help you were looking for!

Students in all schools and at all levels must know that their teacher or professor is in charge. He or she is empowered to execute programs for the benefit of all students. Studies, homework, grades, and monitoring scholastic progress is entrusted to the teacher. Everything you do in the classroom counts towards your final grade. This includes assignments, homework, projects, and classroom participation. Therefore a student must get involved in all class related activities and earnestly comply with all of the course requirements.

Helpful Tips To Students:

- Always present yourself well dressed, groomed, and clean. Be punctual to your classes and appointments. Tardiness will count against you.

- Always greet fellow students and teachers. When your teacher or fellow students greet you always acknowledge and reciprocate.

- Prepare for your classes by completing homework, study assignments, and readings assigned.

- Long term assignments, projects, and classroom related activities have deadlines. Meet those deadlines. Your final grade depends on it.

- If you must have additional time to complete an assignment or project, be sure to explain your situation to your teacher as far in advance of the due date as possible. Never ever wait until the day the project is due to ask for an extension! It will be too late. If you do this and respectfully request a deadline extension, it may be granted to you.

- If you have questions, write them down and ask your teacher after lecture rather than during lecture unless he/ she invites class. Usually you will get more attention after class. Scheduling an appointment with your teacher is also appropriate. Get the advice and guidance you need from the horse's mouth!

- Aside from scheduled quizzes, tests, and projects your teacher may announce a short surprise quiz! This is done to test your compliance with homework and attention to detail in class.

- If you receive lower scores or fewer points than expected, approach your teacher tactfully and respectfully for clarification and explanation. Never argue. Argument over grades is counterproductive.

- Be sure to thank your teacher and fellow students for any help you may receive. Paying back all favors you receive is a sign that you are a sure winner.

- If and when a fellow student drives you to school or home be sure to offer and ask "May I pay you for gas?" or "Just let me split the cost with you." Your friend will admire your offer.

- If you need help with your assignments, homework and laboratory projects your teacher or fellow students may help if you approach them properly.

- When something goes wrong and you caused it, accept full responsibility. If your homework, assignment, and project are incomplete make no excuses. Remember that all students require help from their teachers so get that help at the right time — right when you need it.

- Every student must have a well written resume on hand. A resume is required of you if you plan to pursue a career or higher studies. Floating or circulating your resume has definite advantages. Your updated resume may raise some eyebrows; fetch a dream job or a prized academic position. Therefore upgrade your resume periodically and make it available to people and companies of your choice.

Most foreign students are not quite familiar with the art of resume writing. Your resume developed as described below, can become your first most important step of a long successful career. Your talents, experience, and potentials need to be detailed in print! Therefore do some serious self-examination, reflect on your career/professional goals, education, and expertise. Prepare a summary of what you have studied and accomplished. Make a list of your skills and then spend much time to develop your accurate resume. Study the following simple format and get started with your resume in earnest for your own benefit!

Personal Information

John S. Doe, B.Sc.

Present and permanent address: Must list current address, permanent address if different from current address (optional).

1234 KST Road, 4175 MGM Road,

Bangalore, Karnataka State, Mangalore, Karnataka State,

India- 489831 India- 575410

My phone number: 924-469-1787 Phone Number: 824-428-7897

My E-mail: iloveto_healyou@g.com

Objective:

Your job objective is the most important eye catching phrase that must attract a curious Human Resource Manager. As you come across positions listed in the newspaper or web, you will know the job title for your qualification (s). The job that is most relevant to your training, experience, and education is what you must be after! Decide upon the type of job/position you are seeking.

Suggestions:

- If seeking admission to an undergraduate, graduate or internship program simply state your objective. Please see example 1 below.
- If this is your 1st job search after graduation then see example 2 below. Clearly state that you are seeking the advertised entry level position.

- If you are seeking a professional or management position with an eye on your future, develop a crisp summary of your experience. Highlight your accomplishments in various capacities. See summary below to get that extra traction!

Example:

1. Looking for admission to graduate/internship program in Molecular Biology. It will help your application if you state your specific interest, area of research, and the professor under whom you wish to study.

It is important that you provide background information along with your exceptional grades and GPA in your major subjects.

2. Desire a Research/Teaching position in Molecular Biology with special emphasis on pharmacological influence on specific proteins.

If seeking entry level position in industry such as advertising, banking, and marketing clearly state your intent and provide all necessary information for consideration.

Summary:

It is appropriate to present a summary if you have had several years of experience and you plan to advance your career. Therefore provide a brief summary of your achievements, honors, and awards. You need to highlight critical tasks that profited your employer(s), innovative methods you introduced to cut waste, save money, accomplish greater efficiency, and productivity. You may list honors and awards and publications separately but make sure that they are prominently displayed. Also place a dollar value on all those achievements you bragged so much about!

Education, Training, Licenses, Certifications, And More:

Name of college, university attended. Begin with most recent degree/diploma earned (B.S. / M.Sc.) and years attended. List major subjects (Physics/Chemistry) along with GPA and overall GPA. List minor subjects (English, Accounting) if you see an advantage to do so. Continue to list other colleges and universities attended. List major/

minor subjects studied, years attended, and degree/diploma received. You must list honors, awards, scholarships, and letters of distinction received from each school.

High School Attended:

Name of High School and years attended. Also include a list of your accomplishments, honors, awards (academic and athletic), and scholarships.

Other Training, Certification, Licenses or Military Service:

List special training (Firefighter, First aid), skills (EMT, computer programmer), and licenses (Physical Therapy, Nurse). If you were in the military specify the branch you served.

Experience:

Provide a brief summary of most recent job/title with years worked. Highlight your accomplishments with emphasis on revenue generated, cost cutting measures introduced, and enhanced efficiency and productivity accomplished. Proceed with previous employment/duration with emphasis on results as described above. List all previous jobs/titles along with achievements down to internship. Part time jobs unrelated to desired position should be avoided.

Activities:

List professional activities. These should include professional membership(s), research projects (past and current), field activities, and current interests.

Technical Skills:

This is critical. Carefully list your unique technical skills. Elaborate if necessary (Electron microscopy, Tissue culture techniques, Computer software).

Publications: List all publications in the order published. Most current publication must be at the top.

Hobbies:

List only genuine hobbies (Gardening, Coin collection, Hiking).

References:

List provided upon request. Keep a list of references handy. Make sure the people on the list are aware that they are on your list! You must maintain few lists with alternate references.

University Campus
Winter Look

CHAPTER EIGHT
SEEKING EMPLOYMENT OPPORTUNITIES

Resume Building
Helpful Tips For Your Resume
Preparing For Interviews
Pre-Interview Check-List
Practical Tips For A Good Job Interview

Professional life is a true adventure no matter which corner of the world you are employed in. American executives look for competent personnel who are prepared to go that extra mile. Employees in the United States receive good pay. Most employers offer benefits such as sick leave, health insurance, and vacation pay. The living standards and quality of life in the United States is the envy of the world. That is why many countries experience brain drain! A good paying job in the United States is worth chasing after. Your keen sense, hard work, exceptional communication and negotiating skills are necessary to secure that dream job! Your negotiating skills, attention to detail, and focus on the intricate details of the job itself is what will impress your prospective employer. However once you secure your dream job you must make efforts, work hard, and take precautions to hold on to that job. We have helpful suggestions for job seekers and employees wishing to hold on to that precious job.

In order to secure a position that is appropriate for your qualifications, you must first develop a resume as described in the previous chapter. A truly impressive resume must be attractively presented in a crisp reader friendly format. In essence your resume should be an eye opener. Most Human Resource Managers will likely pick resumes that are attractive, error free, and well written. In addition, a short catchy cover letter that plays up your skills and credentials is an ABSOLUTE MUST! The letter must focus on your potential and explain why you are the right candidate and the best fit for the advertised job.

Universities, colleges, state and local educational institutions guide students in their job search. You will find such information in the campus bulletin boards, fliers, and school newspapers. Most schools promote mentor and networking advantages to their students. You may attend job fairs and seminars sponsored by your school and be ahead of the curve!

Helpful Tips for Your Resume

- The most important part of your resume, your OBJECTIVE must be compatible with your professional training, degree or diploma. It must clearly state your professional goals and aspirations. If you have an impressive professional career, you must develop a summary of your accomplishments and highlight them here as well.
- Always keep your resume accurate, current, and positive.

Upgrade as often as necessary and have a few copies available at all times.

- Type your resume in bold glossy letters; use a professional resume service if necessary. If you prefer to do it yourself, find reference materials on writing your resume in the local public or college library. Refer to multiple sources for the project.

- Be truthful and avoid exaggerations. Your resume must provide all prospective employers a clear picture of your career goals, skills, abilities, and potential.

- Provide a separate list of your references upon request only. Be sure to inform your referees that you have listed them as references.

- Do not list salary requirements. Most jobs have set fixed salaries or salary ranges.

- Spelling, grammar, and typo errors are unacceptable. Proofread and correct your draft. Then proofread and correct again and then proof, proof, and proof, and correct. Ask others too if possible to help you proofread before printing your final version. Your resume should be perfect or nearly so.

- Your resume must list your professional accomplishments and job titles. Listing only duties without accomplishments may not work in your favor. If you have inventions, patents, and other achievements be sure to highlight them. Your accomplishments will open doors for you.

- Certain positions are revenue oriented. If you seek a position in marketing, design or manufacturing be sure to highlight the increased revenue dollars that you were able to generate for your employers. Include a line like, "My marketing/

design/manufacturing skills increased revenues by 20% or a gain of 34 million dollars over a 3 year period."

- If you seek a job in management, point out your money saving skills such as your emphasis on efficiency, ability to reduce and eliminate waste resulting in higher productivity. Point out the results of your creativity to accomplish higher production and increased revenues and add a line such as "The changes I introduced to reduce waste and inefficiency saved my company over 3 million dollars annually."

- Never include your personal details - likes and dislikes. Some candidates prefer to include a recent photograph. Truth be told, many seem to agree! Certain positions may even invite your recent picture! We strongly recommend such a favor be delivered upon request only.

- It is not wise to list part time and summer jobs that are not related to the profession you intend to work in. We recommend that you do so only to demonstrate that your learned skills and talents are necessary for the job at hand.

- Mail/hand deliver your resume along with an eye opening cover letter with return address and day time phone number. If the advertised position is what you are really after, mail or hand deliver your second resume a week later as a reminder. This will show your prospective employer that you are truly interested.

Your resumes if presented as described above should open doors for you and earn invitations for job interviews. Then personal contact is your best opportunity to market you. But be prepared to answer some tough questions such as the following. *"Why should I hire you? What are your weaknesses? Why do you want to quit your present job? What are your salary requirements? Tell me little bit about your current/previous boss/supervisor."*

Then there may be a few "tricky" questions to distract and test your character/temperament. So be ready to be challenged with the unexpected. As the interview progresses and you begin to feel more confident, watch your P's and Q's. This is the time when some candidates become reckless. The interviewer may seize this moment to ask particularly difficult questions such as, *"Why did you leave your last job? What are your requests/demands?"* or *"How would you handle tardiness? What if your coworker requires help or advice? Will you stay overtime if need be? Will you work on weekends?" Can you suggest a solution to our company's overtime problem?"*

Your search for a dream job will come with a tremendous cost requiring sweat and tears. At times you will be frustrated and disappointed. Be prepared to spend much time to overcome the common hurdles of the job hunt by looking for "only jobs you know you are trained, studied and qualified for." Some candidates apply for jobs that they may never qualify! Develop a good strategy that will work best for you. Your strategy will produce desirable results if you implement it with total discipline. Challenge yourself with likely possible interviewer questions and develop meaningful answers. The questions must address issues such as your career goals, potential, interest, salary, and suitable position. With clarity of purpose, your determination to accomplish set goals will help you achieve them. This aggressive approach will save you time and provide an advantage over candidates who also seek interviews in your field. You will eventually have more time to prepare for that all important personal interviews.

Pre-Interview Check-List

- Your appearance is very important therefore groom and present yourself well dressed. Make sure that clothes are freshly laundered and pressed. If your shoes are not new polish the pair you plan to wear. You must pay special attention to matching clothes, tie, shirt, dress, and shoes.

- Body odor, bad breath, untidy hair, and unclipped fingernails are killers! Pay close attention to these details. Use breath fresheners and reliable deodorant. If needed, apply small dabs of cologne/perfume. Be careful, overuse of these products may be counterproductive.

- It's very critical that you know the company/corporation well before you go to interview. Read about and research the company's products/services, market share, financial strength, and the direction in which the company is poised to move in. Your insights into the company will work as a spring board to your advantage as you answer questions.

- Know your interviewer and his/her interests. You may have to use some subtle ways to find these out but its well worth investigating. Such knowledge could help you to carry on an interesting conversation or ice breaker.

- Be friendly. Exude the right kind of chemistry. Smile when it's appropriate and use your body language to deliver your message or emphasize your point.

- Always take a book or a magazine along for reading while waiting for that big event. Show your future employer that you do not waste time!

Your research and thorough preparation for this important event will benefit you and impress your interviewers. Seize this opportunity to overwhelm them and score big. A good first interview will assure you of subsequent interviews and ultimately success in securing the prized job you seek. As you prepare for your first interview, remember that you get only one chance to make a good first impression. Speak softly and politely. As much as possible, make eye contact as you answer questions. It's a make or break moment. It's your best bet and only chance to prove your skills and market you!

Practical Tips for a Good Job Interview

- Know the time/place of your interview, the interviewer's name or the names of those on the interviewing team. The actual interview may last for 30-45 minutes or more in some cases. As a courtesy the interviewer usually will inform you of the approximate length of the interview and how many will be interviewing you. You should be confident and look forward to this opportunity and answer all reasonable questions with enthusiasm and unshakable candor.

- Be punctual to your interview. It's wise and practical to report 10-15 minutes ahead and be seated. If you must hire a cab, call for a cab well in advance (2-4 Hours), not when you are ready to step out of your house! The cab driver should know your destination and number of people riding. Remember to take your briefcase and portfolio even though your team of interviewers already has your resume and references.

- Do not pace nor check your watch for time if you arrive too early. Keep yourself occupied - pull that book or magazine out!

- Do not smoke nor chew gum. If chewing gum, dispose of it with a tissue before the interview.
- Turn OFF your cell phone.
- When interviewers appear briskly stand, greet them with a smile, and a firm handshake. Stand with a pleasant disposition/posture until asked to take your seat. Quickly express thanks for selecting you for this job opportunity and take your seat!
- Let the interviewers begin. Do not interrupt but listen intently. Make eye contact and study their facial expressions/body language while answering questions and making your presentation. Do not show discomfort.
- Keep in mind that this interview is ALL ABOUT YOU! You must skillfully play up your expertise, point out accomplishments and experience in areas critical to the job at hand. Convince the interviewing team that YOU ARE THE BEST FIT. Let them know how well YOU can complement and benefit the new employer – but do not get carried away! Bragging may backfire.
- Keep your answers short and crisp. Do not confuse and create doubt. Do not repeat nor dwell on non-consequential matters. Try not to crack jokes.
- Never volunteer unsolicited information no matter what the circumstances are. Just answer the questions as asked.
- Do not get carried away with humility! Answer all questions in a firm, convincing, polite tone with subtle and appropriate body language. Frequent use of sir and madam is considered "sucking up!"
- Do not carry a demand list nor tell your interviewers what you expect them to do for you. Some applicants demand

vacation, fewer hours, and unusual favors! Even a most desperate employer would have second thoughts about hiring you!

- If and when asked about previous employments make no derogatory comments. It is sufficient to say that you were employed there, enjoyed working for that company, and acquired valuable experience on the job.

- If you had the misfortune of losing your last job for whatever reason, do not blame anyone including yourself! You may want to tell your interviewer that the previous company was downsizing or your departmental jobs were outsourced (if it's true). You may explain to the interviewer what happened (in your opinion) with no anger or pain in your voice. Ignoring and not answering the question may hurt your chances!

- As much as possible do not request interviewer (s) to repeat questions. When not totally comfortable politely ask them for clarification.

- When you are not sure of an answer to a pointed question, it's wise to politely admit it. Proceeding with a wrong answer or making something up is JOB SUICIDE.

- If at the end, you felt you answered a question incorrectly, politely point out that it was an error and quickly correct your answer.

- When the interview is over, you may ask when it would be appropriate to call and inquire if you are selected. Usually the interviewing team leader will volunteer that information to you. However under no circumstances show undue anxiety. When your interview is over leave without delay, do not mull around or ask questions. Doing so will only create a bad impression.

- Always make time to mail "Thank You" notes to all those present at your interview. It's also appropriate to briefly refer to one or two topics discussed during the interview that made it so memorable to you. If this procedure is implemented, you will have impressed everyone involved in your job interview process.

The first successful interview as pleasant and rewarding as it may appear, more often than not is only a small first step. Therefore be prepared to be invited back for a second, third, and more interviews with additional key personnel. Some companies require that all section heads, supervisors, and key decision makers (KDM) provide input into hiring all prospective employees. This process may take several weeks! So be very patient--it will eventually pay off.

CHAPTER NINE
EMPLOYMENT IN THE UNITED STATES

Congratulations! You Got Your Dream Job
Now, Here's How To Keep It......
Tips To Improve Your Job Performance

It's imperative that you realize that your serious efforts are necessary to keep the job that you just bagged. Love of job is not enough. There is a lot more to keeping your job than simply doing a good job and keeping busy. Your attitude, skills, punctuality, organization, and a multitude of other details count for or against you. You will spend a great deal of time on the job interacting with fellow employees therefore it's important that you develop friendship and sound working relationships with them. The work force must function as a team and create a pleasant working environment. Every employee has a responsibility to contribute as much as possible to his/her work place. As a new employee it's incumbent upon you to learn the ropes, adjust, accommodate, and get along with fellow employees. Your good disposition, positive attitude, pleasing social skills, good working habits, ethics, and proper etiquette will make lasting impact on employees you work with and help you become a valuable member of that team.

Life on the job starts on the first day you report to work. Most places of employment have proven successful training programs for new employees. You will meet with your supervisors and fellow employees. Employers also provide education, guidance, and training on various jobs related matters. On time reporting to work, code of conduct, and expected work ethics will also be discussed. You will be informed about your duties, obligations, and rights. There will be in-services and intense training on safety issues, fire drills, and disaster response. Companies that provide unique services may educate and train new employees to cope with special situations they normally handle such as CPR, first aid, and emergency evacuations. You will be paid during this intense initiation period – as per your wage agreement.

Your employer has every reason to believe that you will love your job. It is your responsibility to prove him/her right. Most companies provide an employee handbook which lists company policies, guidelines, regulations, benefits, and acceptable practices on the job. Make extra effort to understand all aspects of your job in explicit detail. Read and reread the handbook, bring the handbook home and reread in the company of your spouse! Make yourself very familiar with your company's policies and procedures on various job related matters. Know what to do and whom to approach at all times especially in cases of emergency, difficult situations, and your professional needs. Know the details of your benefit package such as vacation time, personal leave, sick leave, holiday pay, restrictions, guidelines for overtime pay, provision for maternity leave, and all issues important to you and to your employer.

Your employer has high expectations of you! Therefore report to work on time every time; it will work in your favor. Prove to your supervisor that you are dependable. You must develop and practice appropriate workplace code of conduct for your own benefit from the very outset. Plan not to make excuses. Set your priorities straight. Focus on quality of work with few or no mistakes but don't let productivity suffer! Your professional growth, advancement of your career is too important for you to ignore good work habits.

Some Helpful Tips on Your Career Building:

- Report to work a few minutes (10-15) ahead of starting time. If you must clock in and out, faithfully follow company policy for overtime.

- If you ever run late call your immediate supervisor with the exact cause for the delay such as an accident or traffic jam. Be truthful. Employers do not entertain tardiness. If you expect to be late for work inform your employer ahead – days or week in advance! He/she will appreciate your consideration. If tardiness becomes chronic, chances are your employer will not keep you on the payroll.

- Always be courteous, considerate, and respectful to everyone at work. Greet and acknowledge all coworkers as you arrive at work. Help maintain a happy and pleasant work atmosphere.

- Your job will require your initiation and training from the get go. Your training period is also considered a probationary period. Your employer most likely has a training manual for new recruits. Read and reread the training manual. Know the procedures and be proficient in areas where your expertise is considered critical. Do not hesitate to ask questions. Know that asking questions proves that you are interested but don't get carried away with questions not related to work.

- Apply yourself and pay attention to detail and always remember the details are important. As you prepare to wind down, clock out/call it quits, double check critical areas of your work such as figures, procedures, and the like. Leave your work place clean, free of clutter, and ready for the next shift or your next visit.

- As a new employee (new kid on the block!) watch all your moves, attitude, and your compliance with the new work place practices. Comments such as "I like to do this procedure differently because this is how I did it on my last job", is a sure way to throw your baby with the bathwater!

- As you build your confidence on the job, make time to meet with your supervisor periodically to receive advice and guidance. Solicit his/her opinion about your job performance in order to do better.

- Your supervisor and fellow employees are critical to your success and continued employment. Always look to support them and express your thanks for the support and training you receive.

The following are useful suggestions to heed in a workplace. Follow them as best as you can but remember to adapt to your unique new workplace environment at all times even if it is cumbersome and unpleasant. That is considered positive attitude and having interest and love for your job!

Tips To Improve Your Job Performance

- Your job requires "team effort." Plan and work hard to

become a strong, dependable team member. The team you help build is as strong as the weakest link of the team!

- Keep all discussions and conversations strictly professional. Avoid discussing personal problems with fellow employees on the job. Your medical history, life style, and social life are strictly private and treat them as such.

- If you have a personal problem or a situation that you must discuss with your supervisor, make an appointment. Explain briefly what is bothering you and ask for his/her opinion. Listen to your boss and request suggestions on how to improve your performance – and follow the leader!

- Never lose your cool/temper during your meeting with your boss or fellow employees. You cannot accomplish any of your set goals/targets when angry and upset. Be calm and composed. If you expect some difficulty in stating your case, write down the main points and present your side in a calm determined voice. If necessary be assertive but do not shout.

- Never accuse or degrade fellow employees either in public or in private. Use positive, constructive ways to describe a situation rather than outright criticism. Seek solutions by involving co-workers in a problem-solving process. If there are genuine work-related disagreements, keep them on a professional level while carefully maintaining personal and professional relationships. If you have to - agree to disagree!

- Always maintain the highest standards of integrity and professional conduct. Work hard when you are supposed to.

- Certain tasks require more than 8 hours to complete – if

you ever face a situation such as this, communicate well with your supervisor and coworkers involved so the project is successfully accomplished.

- On occasion you may have to delegate a task or two to your team member. Write a friendly note; explain in detail how to get it done – a phone call also may be appropriate in order to avoid any confusion.

- Do not take money, food, supplies, and other valuables from the company or from other employees. Resist the temptation to use an excuse like "others do it all the time." Just say No! Your employer and coworkers will admire your honesty and integrity.

- Under no circumstances use company time and property for personal gain. Many companies have strict rules. Know and follow the rules to the letter.

- When at work avoid engaging the company phone, fax, and internet for personal business. Employers do not tolerate the use of company computers for personal and non-work related matters.

- Always keep your workplace clean, neat, and organized no matter how busy and overworked you are. It's a good reflection of your pride and commitment to your job!

- Be respectful to all who work with you. A kind word, timely praise, a helping hand, and a few words of support will go a long way. You will earn respect from your coworkers and more so from your supervisor!

- Be sympathetic to workers who have a tough time on the job or elsewhere. Offer advice only if asked. Respect other's privacy. Do not divulge nor share confidential employee information with your comrades and friends on the job or within the company. Show your boss and coworkers that you can be trusted.

- Do not discuss your wage with fellow employees. Remember the saying: "Never ask a man's wage and a woman's age!" You can make the workplace a fun place by taking your job seriously. The benefits are many and the rewards are great.

- Good behavior and attitude may earn you high marks. Remember that quality and quantity of work DOES MATTER! Therefore it is important that you are well organized and accomplish all your tasks on time every time. If on occasion you require more time to get the job done make sure that you stay back and get it done. You will get a pat on the back and earn greater job security.

- If on occasion your boss requests that you stay longer to complete a task or a critical project, gracefully comply. Your boss has a reason to pick you. He trusts the quality of your work over other subordinates. Consider that a feather in your hat!

- Respect company property such as the phone system, computers, machinery, automobiles, uniforms, common areas, and rest rooms. Company property is valuable!

It is expected of an employee to adhere to company policies, guidelines, and set standards. You must quickly learn the do's and don'ts, work ethics, and expected behaviors for your job. As there may be rewards for exceptional achievement, there may be also harsh punishment for lack of compliance. After spending months trying to secure your dream job, you would be terribly disappointed if you were to lose it. This Guide has tips to avoid such tragic episodes. We have listed below some common mistakes employees make on the job.

Most Common Pitfalls Endangering The Security Of Your Employment:

- Not supporting your "team" on the job and refusing to comply with company policies, rules, and standards.
- Not reporting to work on time or ahead of time. No employer will tolerate chronic tardiness and unreliable help.
- Not learning the job from the outset. Know what and how much is expected of you. Have the discipline to adhere strictly to the guidelines, policies, procedures, and the deadlines.
- Refusing to learn new methods/procedures. This is a sure killer! New and innovative ways to conduct business help your company. Take a keen interest in promoting innovation!
- Sub-standard job performance causing delays in product delivery.
- Willfully abusing company time, equipment, technology, and computers. Company time is valuable as well as its' technology and equipment. When employees misuse them, overall productivity and morale slip!
- Having a poor attitude, frequently making complaints and excuses to justify inappropriate behavior. People on the job need to focus and perform at optimum pace so the goods and services may be delivered on time all the time.
- Engaging in and encouraging gossip. Not being a team player on the job. Unreliable employees are burdens rather than assets. Such individuals often bring disrepute, poor morale; disrupt teamwork, and work-flow.

- Not keeping your religious and political affiliations strictly private.
- Sharing information about your family, social, sex, personal, and night life with fellow employees may result in unintended consequences.
- Carrying on personal business/affairs at work. Inviting friends to the job site.
- Personal phone calls, shopping, and internet related entertainment.
- Not placing company's interests above your personal interests. Be part of a strong team. Remember the phrase "United we succeed and divided we fall." You must make a difference for your company and your employer.
- Willfully wasting time, carrying on conversation unrelated to work, disregarding priorities, and ignoring deadlines may hurt your job security and chances for advancement.
- Stealing the spotlight from your boss even though you may have had more to contribute to the project's success than your boss. Show him/her respect at all times especially in the presence of his/her boss. Your boss as the head of your department deserves full credit for his team's accomplishments.
- You have earned and deserve vacation time. But your team needs your consideration and contribution when it's crunch time. Not planning ahead and taking your vacation when your services are most required is a NO NO!
- Not maintaining confidentiality if your boss chooses to confide and share with you certain job related matters involving other employees. Such a trustworthy relationship

with your boss is a great asset; betrayal of that trust may cost you a well-deserved promotion and even job security.

- Dishonesty is suicidal. Padding expense accounts, cheating, stealing company property, and misbehavior certainly force your employer to show you the exit door!

A loyal employee is an asset to a company. You must be well aware that in the public eye you represent the company's values and high standards. Therefore it is expected that you make every effort to comply, perform, and excel. Promoting and propagating your company's goals and values is your mission that will benefit your employer. But there is more to that --- you will earn appreciation, job security, trust, and respect from your comrades and "THE BOSS."

CHAPTER TEN
LEARNING AND ADAPTING TO THE AMERICAN WORKPLACE

Workplace In The United States
Changing Your Job
It's Time For A Raise... Here's The Solution

United States is the most developed and industrialized country in the world. American entrepreneurs, supported by the skilled, hard-working, disciplined labor-force made it all possible! Modern day America also has many aggressive, creative, and innovative world famous leaders in business, education, and industry. You will learn much about these men and women as you become familiar with current events via television, radio, and mass media in the United States.

Among the developed nations of the world, United States has the highest paid skilled labor force. Almost all offices, industries, manufacturing plants, and supermarkets are totally automated or nearly so. Working conditions in every sector of the industry in the United States are a matter of national pride. Many American corporations conduct business and provide services here and abroad. This has encouraged thousands of talented men and women from all over the world to seek employment in the United States or with United States' multinational corporations.

This chapter also deals with good working habits, work ethics, and etiquettes on the job. Our goal is to make you aware of the environment and atmosphere that you are likely to experience in a workplace in the United States. Business, professional, and academic careers in the United States as in other parts of the world require tremendous personal motivation, patience, and drive if you are to succeed. If employed in the United States, you will most certainly work just like the Americans! You will follow the conventional wisdom "When in Rome do as the Romans do." Employers in the United States are quite demanding and result oriented. They expect discipline, greater output, and quality work! Many work-places have signs posted that says it all – "Work smart not hard!" This requires keen interest and commitment to your job. Therefore be prepared to learn, adapt, and comply with a totally different work environment and culture in the United States! If you do so with diligence you will be much appreciated and of course handsomely rewarded!

Workplace atmosphere and culture in the United States is unique in many ways - it's very informal, cordial, and relaxed. It is designed to promote team spirit, efficiency, organization, and productivity. Therefore make much effort to learn about your new job with the company in the United States and apply what you learned from get go. Ignoring company rules and guidelines may adversely affect your chances to achieve your professional cum financial goals. Security of your coveted job may also be at stake! Your proficient professional job skills, pleasant manners, consideration of others at work, work ethics, and above all your learned American work habits will help you stay on the job. The professional and personal impact you make will ultimately earn you the job security you're looking for.

You must understand that to be part of the American work force you require exceptional professional skills, training, and some experience. Of course you require a degree or diploma in the required field as well. You must also know that employees in the United States are very familiar with office, laboratory and industrial automation, cutting edge technology, and state of the art advances in their specialty. In fact, the labor-force in the United States will be lost without it! The automation explosion is a buzz word for all labor and work related activity in the United States. Employers in the United States expect you to be familiar with modern machinery and advanced technologies in your profession. No matter what your training, specialization, and interest you must be proficient in automation in every aspect of your job. Your operational talents coupled with troubleshooting skills will make you a much sought after professional.

Workplace In The United States

Almost all large and not so large cities in the United States are modern. Tall multi-story buildings, attractive architecture, and high tech amenities are breathtaking to say the least! You will find ultra-modern offices equipped with telephones, computers, copiers, fax machines, and other gadgets for the convenience of customers and employees. All these buildings are equipped with heating and cooling systems for winter and summer.

Foreign professionals seeking employment in the United States are mostly educators, engineers, physicians, scientists, and skilled technicians. Educators, scientists, and technicians usually prefer employment with colleges, universities, and research centers. Engineers and technicians look for assembly plants, factories, industry, manufacturing, and processing outfits. Physicians naturally choose employment with clinics, hospitals, and healthcare facilities.

If you are accepted for employment in your profession you will most likely find your office and place of work in a modern facility as described above. The building will have all the modern gadgets such as smoke detectors, fire alarms, sprinkler system, fire extinguishers, heating and cooling (central air) just to name a few! Make yourself familiar with all the systems and know how to respond during emergency.

Most places of work described above may also have built in gift shops, cafeteria, library, fitness center, and much more for the benefit of employees and visitors. Use these services wisely as per company policies and guidelines.

Now you have a picture of an ideal workplace in the United States! Think of you with all the supporting staff, your supervisor, and coworkers in a busy, highly automated work environment. Most definitely workplace atmosphere in your company is cordial that promotes team spirit. A strong team is sure to achieve set targets with ease. This is the main reason why agricultural and industrial output in the United States is several folds greater than countries with minimum or no automation at all! All sectors of American industry from agriculture to sophisticated weaponry are geared to produce more with minimal labor in less time. Thanks to automation explosion!

Your job offers professional enhancement, financial security, and a future for you and your family. You owe it to yourself and your family to perform well on the job. If you are serious about your job in the United States, you must know that you have to follow company procedures, expected code of conduct and above all solid work ethics - that's what your boss expects. You are also expected to carry your weight and not be too dependent on others to get your job done. Many immigrants make light of American work ethics and engage in conduct and dialogue that's less conducive to good working environment. While on the job in order to keep your job do your job! That's the responsible thing to do. Learn and excel in every aspect and detail of your job. Your job security, professional success, career enhancement, and your family's welfare depend on it.

Helpful Tips To Be A Good Employee:

- Be a smart team player. Become an integral part of a strong team. Learn/develop good social skills and work ethics. Your character and pleasing manners will earn many friends. One feather at a time!
- Americans are immensely patriotic. They love their country just like you love your homeland. Never put America or your country down. Be pragmatic in your opinions about the United States and your country of birth.
- Know that to many Americans, the United States is the only super power. Try not to challenge or disagree with them on this.
- As much as possible be familiar with American history, geography, landscape, customs, and culture. Firsthand knowledge of places of interest and attractions will enhance your ability to engage with friends, fellow employees, and neighbors in interesting conversation! Prove that "Johny can read!"
- It is wise to avoid political, race, and religious discourse. When such topics come up patiently listen, learn, and ask questions so you understand. Be extra careful if and when

you share or dispense opinions on American politics or government policies.

- Take pride in educating your American friends about your homeland with special emphasis on things for which it's globally recognized such as history, tourism, natural wonders, and the like.

- Americans frown at friends and acquaintances looking to borrow money. Always rely on your local bank for this confidential financial transaction. Follow the ancient wisdom: "Never borrow nor lend" if you care to maintain your friendship and good relations.

- Americans believe in self-help and coffee breaks. When opportunity presents always pour a cup for your supervisor, coworker, and then one for yourself. Do not forget to clean your cup and utensils before you leave. All will appreciate your consideration.

- When you open doors in and out of the buildings look around for people in front and behind you. It's courteous and good manners to hold the door for others. When others hold the door for you, express your thanks.

- This is the age of cell phones. Everyone has one. However there are times and places where the phone must be turned off. Your cell phone must be turned off while you are on the job unless your job requires otherwise! No employer in the United States will allow you to entertain incoming or outgoing personal telephone calls.

- When calling coworkers, supervisors, acquaintances or anyone by phone, always identify you first. The person on the other end may not recognize you by your voice. As you terminate your phone conversation thank the person and indicate that you will disconnect. Do not abruptly end the conversation - it's not polite. Good telephone manners always produce favorable results.

- Do not carry on a conversation with food or drink in your mouth.
- If you are a smoker and it's time for smoke, excuse yourself. If you are in a group meeting, conference, seminars, or a serious work related matter, think twice before you excuse yourself! Your coworkers will admire your presence and uninterrupted participation.
- Be kind and considerate to your friends and coworkers at all times. A kind deed always pays off. Volunteer to go the extra mile to help your coworker if an opportunity presents.
- If you don't understand something that is work related, confused about certain procedure or process, politely request your coworker's help. If you are still not sure, it's wise to talk to your supervisor.
- Americans love holidays and long weekends. These are the occasions they look forward to. If your coworkers decide to go away for long weekends accommodate them as much as possible. Do not insist that you too need a long weekend. Your turn will come as you earn seniority!
- Complaining and gossip on or off the workplace is a NO... NO. All your work related issues must be shared in private with your supervisor.
- Foul, demeaning, reckless, and rude expressions will quickly catch up with you. Watch your language and the audience at all times!

Life on the job in the United States is different and much more complex than in any other country of the world. Basic knowledge of

American workplace, good manners, and etiquette for all important or not-so-important occasions is absolutely necessary if you are to get the most out of your time living and working in the United States.

Changing Your Job – What You Must Know

Almost all employees will change jobs for more money, better working conditions, fancy title, and attractive benefits. Some employees choose convenience of walking to work or a shorter ride over material gains. Some employees prefer to work for large corporations or a well-known company. Changing your job may work as a double edged sword! While many will enjoy the change, some may live to regret it! In order to be happy and avoid the latter you must be cautious, diligent, and above all very patient. You would much rather work for a known devil than an unknown one!

As a good and valuable employee, you owe it to yourself to advance your career and financial goals. As a matter of fact you must make that a priority! Therefore always keep your ears to the ground, entertain prospective job opportunities, promotions, and aggressively seek and accept the position that meets most if not all of your professional and financial goals.

Few Helpful Tips When Looking For A New Job:

- You must be certain that changing job will do you much good. So do not let anyone convince you otherwise! This rule will apply if you seek a promotion also!
- Once your mind is made up and you begin to entertain interviews and follow-ups, plan not to share details with anyone but your spouse and family. Your current employer

may not take this news lightly and you may not be prepared for unintended consequences!

- If and when a great job offer is on the table make time to study and restudy every aspect, clause, and conditions attached to the offer. This must include issues such as pay, job title, benefit package, vacation, bonus, probationary period, raises, and all other relevant details bar none! Discuss these critically important matters with your spouse, family, and trusted friends.
- We suggest that you make a list of pros and cons, debate, and then arrive at a decision that is best for your long term goals.
- If the new employer expects a counter-proposal, carefully draft and redraft a counter that is very similar with minor changes. Patiently and skillfully negotiate all aspects of your employment, wage, and other benefits. An outrageous counter will not work in your favor!
- Accept the new job only if you are completely satisfied with all the important details such as pay, benefits, job title, and the like.
- Meet with your new employer, request and receive your appointment letter with mutually acceptable starting date.

You may be anxious to start your new job! But your current employer deserves to know your plans. It's wise to give your employer much time and enough advance notice so your replacement can be found! We insist that you follow company procedures and guidelines for this very important move! Therefore at your very earliest make an appointment with your immediate supervisor and any other individual(s) who must be informed about your departure. Calmly and tactfully inform them that you have decided to resign. We also recommend that you write a formal resignation letter clearly indicating the last day that you will report to work. It's quite appropriate to thank and express appreciation for their support and consideration while you were employed there. You may also point out individuals who made your work interesting and a learning experience. Under no circumstances indicate your displeasure (if any) or lack of interest in the company or the job. Let them know how much he enjoyed and benefited working with them for the company. It's not wise to brag about the job offer at hand – that may offend your current employer!

Your current employer may be reluctant to let you go! He/she may insist that you stay and grow with the company. You may be offered more money, greater incentives, attractive title and the like. You may be caught between a rock and a hard place! A dilemma of this kind as pleasant as it appears must be carefully avoided. The following suggestions will guide you when it's time to make that move gracefully.

- Remember that leaving a job that you enjoy is not always easy: it's very stressful. You will also miss that great team, daily routine, and a working environment that you're so much used to!
- You may have to learn and relearn many new techniques, procedures, and adapt to new work place.
- New job also means new team, new boss, and above all entirely new work- environment!
- Your professional/career advancement is very important and must be pursued at considerable inconvenience!
- Your new job has a greater potential for learning and advancement.
- Changing your mind for a better offer from the current employer may also backfire – so be careful!
- Make this VERY IMPORTANT decision with utmost care

– remember the saying "haste makes waste" – so make time, relax, and decide on the NEW job or the BIG promotion like a pro!

You are skillful, expect the change, and ready to embrace the inevitable! Your mind is made up to move on to the greener pastures, test your limits, and accept the challenge. You are totally convinced that the new job/promotion is what you truly want. The new job offer is a vertical move and not a horizontal one! Therefore you must inform your current employer that you will not entertain any incentives or inducements at this time but certainly keep them in mind. You must do so with great skill and sincerity. A short "Thank You" letter must be mailed after reconsidering the generous offer. It's much to your advantage not to burn the bridges as you depart - continue the friendly relationship - it will pay off in the long run.

Once your resignation is accepted you're still responsible to report to work on time and perform like before! We recommend that you pay greater attention to details, spend much time to train your replacement (if allowed), and plan to complete all projects and assignments before the last day of work. If any of the projects or procedures need additional time leave elaborate notes and instructions to the person taking your place. Consider the following tips and earn goodwill as you say goodbye to your beloved boss and the team.

- Report to work on time or ahead of time until the very last day of work.
- Make time to keep all work-related information in order. All work and procedure manuals must be readily available and prominently displayed.
- All logs and reports must be clearly marked and organized. All reagents, materials, and accessories must be available along with ordering instructions!

- All work-related equipment and instrumentation must be in working order. Regular and preventive maintenance logs must be current along with daily quality control data.
- Keep all manuals and troubleshooting guides current and available for your replacement!
- If work is pending on any project or procedure, invite your boss and your replacement for a meeting and go over the process in detail. You must leave clear written instructions so the project may be completed on time with no hiccups!
- Plan to report to work and be on the job until the last minute of the last day – you will earn much appreciation, respect, and many friends!
- If called upon to help in areas of your expertise after your departure, be receptive - do not show displeasure. Offer to help if possible and let them know that you will welcome such a relationship but have this discussion with your new boss and obtain his wholehearted consent!

At times you may be forced to resign your new found "great job" for reasons beyond your control. You may have had high expectations, false hopes, or just wrong take about the position and duties. And then you may walk into a situation where the new employer may have made an error in selecting you for the advertised slot. Rather than admit the mistake gracefully he/she may look for ways to force you out! While you may be responsible for the former situation, you certainly deserve no credit for the latter! These situations may be rare but the harsh realities of such events brings untold misery, discomfort, and harm to all concerned especially your family and your future professional career. Therefore we recommend that you accept entry level or higher positions after a very thorough and careful consideration of all relevant factors including personal and professional concerns. More money should not be the only criteria to walk into a lion's den!

It's Time For A Raise..... Here's The Solution

Almost all employers in the United States develop and follow certain standards, guidelines, rules, and regulations for the benefit of their staff and employees. They also spell out mutual obligations in the Company Handbook! Federal and State governments closely monitor and guide businesses help deal with employees fairly and according to law of the land. This government oversight has helped employers and employees on several important job-related matters. One such issue is pay! You may be offered a salary or an hourly wage based on your skill and professional training. Employers are encouraged to evaluate employee performance periodically - usually once a year. Employees who perform well are usually rewarded with a pay raise, bonus, and other incentives. Some employees receive education and additional training in order to perform better.

At times an employee may feel that he/she deserves a pay-hike or that's overdue. In some instances an employee may be just too desperate and needs additional dollars. When faced with situations just described consider a meeting with your supervisor. You may suggest such a meeting over a cup of coffee or lunch away from the workplace in order to receive uninterrupted attention. The meeting also must be totally confidential! We suggest that you prepare a short persuasive presentation outlining your reasons to deserve the raise and why it's so important for you at this time. Speak softly and slowly with heavy focus on your job performance so you may be able to extract an answer or a firm commitment in your favor. As you prepare for the meeting keep the following in mind at all times.

- You must present yourself well with a firm handshake and a smile.

- Take your seat directly facing your supervisor and make yourself comfortable. Pay close attention to his/her facial expression and body language!

- Remind yourself and your supervisor the confidential nature of the meeting – no one has to know the details much less the reasons.

- Remember that the meeting is all about YOU! Play up your accomplishments such as quality/quantity of work, revenue enhancement plans, PR skills, and above all dependability and loyalty.

- Most likely your supervisor will initiate the conversation. Respond with a smile and quickly get to the point.

- Keep your voice low, soft, and pleasant but stay the course! You want to impress upon your supervisor why it's critical that you receive more money - bluntly state your reasons as described above. Your mounting bills, unexpected expenses, cost of living, and the like will not get you the raise you deserve! Of course you are a terrific employee with good work habits and excellent job skills – your boss needs to know that you're a go getter!

- It's helpful to point out situations where your exceptional skills made the difference. If you helped your employer generate more revenue, point out additional dollars generated or saved per year.

- If your communication or social skills produced more

business by attracting new clients or retaining existing customers give specific examples.

- It's neither helpful nor advisable to point out your fellow employees wage to justify your request – it's irrelevant and counterproductive!

- Most likely your supervisor is impressed and will take up your cause with his boss or the Human Resource Manager. He/she may recommend a raise by repeating the specifics that you brought to the meeting!

- You will be notified in writing or via another brief meeting with your supervisor. Make time to thank your supervisor in person and then mail a "Thank You" note.

- If for some reason you failed to receive a good raise or less than what you anticipated do not show displeasure – it may send wrong signals. Express your thanks as described above!

There are no easy solutions to some of the thorny job-related issues involving money! Each situation is uniquely different and requires careful attention. Make much effort to avoid unpleasant episodes by maintaining good communication with your immediate supervisor. Coworkers and members of your team need not know about your financial problems. Pay-raise is a personal matter. Protect your interests and nurture that good relationship with your boss. Show him/her that you are trustworthy! Your exemplary attitude and job performance must impress everyone!

This Guide has attempted to address various socially expected behaviors on the job in very specific detail. All situations you may encounter cannot possibly be anticipated nor documented here. You will walk into numerous situations that may well be unique to you. Learn to deal with each situation with your interest and long term goals in mind. Treat everyone on the job with patience, respect, and an open mind. If you do so, you will earn many friends. Moreover, your stay in the United States will be an enjoyable experience that you will long remember fondly.

CHAPTER ELEVEN
BUSINESS OWNERSHIP

Starting A Business
Buying An Existing Business
Selling Your Business

Many immigrants to the United States are anxious to start or buy an existing business. You may be interested in a business such as computer hardware or software service, accounting/tax service, clinic, gift/grocery outfit, manufacturing plant or restaurant. All the above endeavors require unique skills, expertise, and above all hard work to succeed. Possessing a thorough knowledge of all your products and services is very critical. Excellent communication skills, attention to detail, as well as the validity and reliability of the products and services offered are absolutely essential if you are to grow and expand your chosen business and enterprise. The pride and freedom of business ownership is not accessible to ordinary citizens in many countries of the world but it is easily accomplished in the United States.

There are many incentives and great opportunities to potential entrepreneurs in the United States. You must decide the kind of business you want to start or buy for a truly rewarding experience. You have absolute freedom! You need not clock in and out, explain tardiness, ask for vacation time, days off, and increase in your wage! As an ambitious entrepreneur, you chart and navigate the future course of your business. You also define your immediate and long term goals such as revenue generation, expansion of your business, addition/deletion of products/services, hiring new employees, and eliminating the weak links in your work force. As you strive and succeed so will your business.

Entrepreneurship requires capital and plenty of it. When you are ready to start a business you may consider a bank loan for all or partial capital requirement. The bank may lend the requested capital to you based on your unique business plan, credit score, and credit history. Once you are pre-approved for a loan you must do diligent studies of the business. Every aspect of the business bar none must be studied in detail. It is likely that your business idea and plans are professionally sound. But there is more to starting a business! Besides anticipated capital investment, you require physical space (location), labor force, marketing strategies, accounting, and legal expertise. The business plan must recognize the state of the economy, potential market share, payroll, new trends, competition, and anticipated customer base.

When Starting A Business Keep The Following in Mind:

- You must have a thorough knowledge of all aspects of your business such as products/services offered, demand for products/services, procedures, and consulting practices.
- Estimated capital requirement to start and operate your dream business. While over-capitalizing is an advantage

under-capitalizing your business may deny projected exponential growth and very survival of it!

- Know your client base and also frequent users/buyers of your products/services.
- You should choose a convenient location for the physical plant. The location must be easy to reach and accessible to vehicular traffic.
- Integrity, consistency, public relations, marketing, and reliability are the most important ingredients for anticipated/ projected growth of your business.
- Once you choose to start/buy/own a business, employ professionals to represent you to negotiate and finalize details such as proposals, agreements, conditions, and remedies. Hiring a competent accountant and an experienced attorney to work on your behalf would be good first steps.
- Good record keeping, inventory control, professional labor force, customer relations, and client services are critical factors to grow and expand your business.
- No business will survive with an "anything goes" attitude. You must pay careful attention to detail, promote efficiency, and aggressively sell your products and services.
- You must also build relationships with your customers, gain their trust, and deliver all that you promise on time every time.
- An astute business person must also know the competition, market trends, and pricing structure.
- Always maintain high standards and current technology to service your clients. This will give you an edge over your competition!

If an opportunity knocks and you decide to buy an existing business develop a plan for acquisition. The plan must include experts and professionals in every stage of the proposed venture. Make a formal offer only when you are completely satisfied with the detailed study/evaluation/appraisal of the business of your interest. Do not rely heavily on marketing and sales managers! You owe it to yourself to do all the leg work with your thinking cap on! Your proposal must be well written in an attractive format. Even a desperate seller will not entertain a shabby proposal - image counts!

Important Facts To Know If Buying An Existing Business:

- Most important factor and driving force behind buying an existing business clearly and obviously dictated by the current demand and the market share for the products and services the company of your interest provides. The current demand for products/services may not hold true for the future! A realistic projected future demand must be seriously taken into account. You wouldn't be caught selling antiques!

- Size of business, total annual gross income, profit and loss for 3-5 previous years. Annual/monthly operating cost and net profit from federal and state tax returns.

- Number of employees, Key decision makers (KDM), and how many will stay on board with you in the event of a purchase.

- Number of owners/partners who wish to stay on to provide smooth transition and continued customer support.

- Monthly payroll, taxes (local, state, and federal), and other obligations such as unemployment, workman's compensation, insurance, leases, licenses, automobiles, and monthly utility expenses.

- All/any previous, current, and pending contracts with clients, venders, lease holders, and service providers.
- Complete client list and side agreements with clients if any.
- Any verbal agreements with clients, venders, and other service providers.
- Any ongoing or pending court/legal cases. Employment related grievances reported such as workmen's compensation, payroll disputes, sexual harassment, and discrimination matters.
- Previous/current/pending litigations if any. Have your attorney confirm this!
- All/any unpaid, unresolved accounts are seller's responsibility! Your accountant should be checking this out!
- City, county, and state liens on the premises or on the business itself.

The kind/type of specialty business you wish to acquire may have a few other requirements to consider. Your attorney and accountant should be your guides. If you wish to utilize the services of current owners/partners in your venture, you must develop an employment agreement with a no compete clause so you have the benefit of uninterrupted professional support, total projected business volume, account activity, and cash flow.

Investors always look to acquire thriving "gold mines." The common saying that all businesses are for sale to the highest bidder is true. Therefore do not discourage an interested party or refuse dialog with a not so serious party. Business owners reap the benefits of their labor at the time their company is sold for a premium. Just like buying a business requires diligent homework, selling requires even more tough choices, and lots of genuine patience.

Some Useful Tips To Sell Your Profitable Business:

- There is nothing wrong with selling your dream business! If the price is right entertain a serious offer.
- Before you make a commitment on a sale price have a professional evaluate/appraise the entire business in order to fix a reasonable market value.
- Consult your accountant and attorney on all issues especially your expectations, liabilities, and responsibilities.
- Some owners prefer to work for buyers. If this is the case, develop your detailed job description, employment agreement, and stick to it.
- Buyers of certain specialty enterprises/stores expect a non-compete agreement. A poorly executed non-compete agreement may ruin your family's future. Your attorney should educate and guide you to prepare this valuable document.
- Do not presume the buyer is your friend. You must realize it is a business transaction. Therefore know what you must get out of selling your company. Your financial security, family's future, and your planned retirement require careful attention. Leave no room for regrets by taking unnecessary risks.
- The execution of sale with all covenants must be treated with great care. There should be no room for doubts and second

guessing. A sound legal instrument (deed) will protect your interests and future!

- Buyer may request that you carry the loan or guarantee the loan through your bank. Even a desperate seller should have second thoughts!

Many business owners suffer the consequences of a poorly executed sale of their business. It is a disservice to themselves and to their loved ones. Therefore every effort must be made to seek out individuals with expertise in marketing and selling your business. Every clause, condition, covenant, remedies, and other critical details must be ironed out before the "deal is sealed." A well-deserved happy retirement along with your peace of mind may be achieved if you do a little extra home work. Know that selling your business is very involved and needs a great deal of your attention to details. In order to avoid undesirable consequences you must dutifully apply yourself to the careful consideration of all steps in this process.

CHAPTER TWELVE
FAMILY LIFE IN THE UNITED STATES

Love Thy Neighbors!
Buying or Selling Your Home
Food, Finances, And Transport

Family - the society's most basic unit is the oldest, most respected, and honored human institution. A society is comprised of many families. A normal family usually consists of a father, mother, and children. In most societies the father is the head of the household (patriarchal) but a few societies have matriarchal form of families. In this practice the mother is the head of the household. The accepted norm in the Western countries is for an equalitarian system of family organization. Most families in the United States practice this system. There is no "boss" but parents are equal partners under this practice. The parents share the responsibilities, problems, joy of caring, raising, and educating their children. Most American parents rarely exercise authority over their children rather allow them to express their opinions, desires, likes, and dislikes. However parents in the United States also place a higher value on discipline, punctuality, self-help, and sharing of labor. Everyone in the American household is assigned a duty – such as loading and emptying the dishwasher, cleaning, garbage disposal and yard work.

American families, like families all over the world aspire for a good, happy, comfortable life. A home with latest modern conveniences is just the beginning. Americans look for all these and much more! Families in the United States love to live in big castles with pets, beautiful lawn, and all the luxuries. A vast majority of Americans own homes with two, three, and more bedrooms. They also own land surrounding their home. A piece of America! More families and individuals own property in America than in any other country in the world. The convenience of home ownership encourages families to live and enjoy life their way.

A modern American home is usually equipped with telephone, television, computer system, central air, hot water, washer, dryer, dishwasher, microwave, and much more. Most households have one or more automobiles. Many Americans have pets such as dogs, cats, birds, fish, and other exotic animals. Most American homes have decorative indoor plants, conversation pieces, and novelty knick knacks. Almost all homes and dwellings in the United States are decorated with fine carpet, rugs, and other accessories.

The American Dream is to hold a good job, to build or buy and live in a beautiful home – a home with many modern amenities as described above! Buying a home is a huge investment - the largest that you would ever make. If you are fortunate enough to own your own home, then you must take every precaution to preserve and appreciate your home's value. You must take care of the yard, cut the grass regularly, keep flower beds live and attractive, prune trees and shrubs as needed. Your dream home must look as good as your next door neighbor's if not better! Keeping your home well maintained and attractive should be a matter of pride. Your dream home will provide desired comforts and an ideal environment to raise and rear your children. With a home and family also come neighbors! Homeowners routinely encounter and deal with frequent distractions from the door bell ringing, dogs barking, and myriad other situations! This requires patience and enormous social skill!

This Guide has some practical tips for you to enjoy your beautiful home. As neighbors are an important part of residential living, the following tips will help you to develop and share neighborly love and friendship. As you review these suggestions keep in mind that people and occasions vary from time to time and place to place. Not all suggestions will work for all situations with all neighbors!

Recommended Neighborly Tips:

- Always greet your neighbors appropriately ("Good morning," "Good evening,") when and if you run into them.
- Never invite yourself or your family over to your neighbor's yard or home. Spare the surprise!
- Invite your neighbors only for special occasions such as block parties, picnics, cook-outs, games, and the like. Once you know each other well you may invite them for other events. Gradual, progressive relationships are healthy.
- End your parties at a reasonable hour so your neighbors may have peace and quiet.
- Yelling, screaming, or ranting obscene language is a "NO... NO." Even if you may be tempted to justify by claiming "It's in the family."
- Offer to help with their garden or yard if your neighbors inform you that they will be away or out on vacation. Your neighbors may request your help with garbage, newspaper,

mail collection, watering indoor plants, or other chores. Help them if you can.

- Manage and maintain your yard just like your neighbors! Keep flower beds attractive, prune trees and shrubs as needed. Always keep your yard clutter and weed free.

- Plan your purchases of food, beverages, and supplies for your household so as not to run out and cause you to borrow from your neighbors. If you must borrow items such as lawn mower, hose, rake, clippers, and the like be sure to return them on time. If an item you borrowed gets damaged insist upon replacing it at your expense. Remember to return the favor and offer to loan any similar items to your neighbor if he/she needs them.

- If your child or pet breaks or damages neighbor's property or valuables first offer apologies and then replace damaged/broken items.

- On occasion you may be asked to accept babysitting service but be extremely careful. If you have no experience admit it and politely decline. Offer or accept to take care of your neighbor's pet(s) only if you have interest, time, and experience.

- Never expect or demand any favor or services from your neighbors. But accept them gracefully if offered. Never borrow nor lend automobile, boat, jewelry, money, and the like – it's a huge risk!

- A common sense approach in dealing with common driveways, lawn, trees, plants, and shrubs will have long and lasting benefits. Place a higher value on maintaining good relations with your neighbors.

- When in neighbor's house behave appropriately. Do not

smoke unless allowed. Avoid walking in with dirty shoes, open containers of food, drinks, and beverages.

- If you are the newest family in the neighborhood make a point to meet neighbors when possible either outside the house, at church, synagogue, school, or supermarket. Ringing the doorbell may annoy some.

- When new neighbors move in and settle down, send a card introducing yourself and your family. If you have the misfortune of having a neighbor who does not reciprocate or appreciate your well-meaning gesture, worry not! Ignoring them is not the solution. Treat them as if they are your best friends but know to stay away until they choose otherwise. Do not impose or be a pest.

- Never discuss matters not related to yourself and your neighbor. Gossip will quickly catch up with you and turn off friends and neighbors.

- There may be unfortunate situations such as accidents, deaths, and misfortunes in the neighborhood. Be sensitive and offer appropriate greetings or words of comfort. It's also a thoughtful gesture to send a card for the occasion. Your neighbor will surely appreciate that you care and share their grief.

- Your neighbors will appreciate receiving greetings for occasions such as Christmas, birthdays, graduations, or any other special occasion. It's very thoughtful, appropriate, and neighborly!

- Remember the Jones's! Keep your yard, driveway, and home (inside and out) always clean and attractive. Your neighbors will thank you. Know how to maintain your lawn weed free. A well maintained home with attractive weed free lawn appreciates in value. A well-kept attractive home creates a good impression. It also reflects well on you, you're family, and your neighborhood.

American families adopt a unique approach to their residential preferences. They will relocate to a new home for various reasons such as to be closer to work, to have a shorter distance to school, church, or simply to live in a new or more desirable neighborhood. Moving also involves selling your existing home and buying another one. A potential home buyer or seller should engage a professional real estate service for this purpose. A reputable real estate company, a well-qualified agent with sound credentials and references is a huge advantage. Home buying and selling requires time, patience, and a caring professional who will serve you well. If you are selling your home, your Real Estate Agent may request you to comply with a check list such as cleaning the house, tastefully decorating the house, and fixing any eye catching sore issues in and around the house. Conversely if you are looking to buy your dream home prepare a check list of all qualities your new house must have and adhere to it. The check list should be prepared jointly by you and your knowledgeable Real Estate Agent.

You will find listings of professional real estate services in every local telephone directory, newspapers, yellow pages, and the Web. However whether buying or selling your home rely heavily on yourself by doing necessary research such as finding out the current market value, current and future demand, and available amenities. The potential for appreciation of home's value is also a very important consideration when buying your new home. Whether buying or selling your home, engage an experienced attorney, follow his advice, and enjoy peace of mind! Your attorney will educate and guide you about the local and county restrictions and guidelines.

Buying Or Selling Your Home:

- When you are ready to buy or sell your home, contact an experienced attorney. This must be done before you execute the purchase or sale agreement!
- Attorney must examine the property in question for any physical or hidden defects, zoning regulations, easements, and restrictions.
- Your attorney must guide you in matters such as taxes, special assessments, mechanics' liens, and other monetary liens against the property.
- The property must be inspected by licensed professionals before closing. This must include the roof, foundation, structure, electric, plumbing, and all appliances.
- A "marketable" title and a "clean" deed is what you must have in order to qualify and receive required financing from the lender!
- The possession of the property, terms of payment, and other issues related to the transaction must be approved by your attorney before you sign on those dotted lines!

Buying or selling your home is a monumental task requiring patience, perseverance, and hard work. The real estate laws vary from state to state and communities in the United States! Your careful attention to detail and a competent attorney on your side is an absolute must to accomplish this very complex transaction.

Some immigrants to America need to acquire new skills or adapt themselves to ways that are unique to living in the United States. Many American men cook one or more daily meals, help clean the house, mind children, and do laundry! Men also manage the household, shop for groceries, and balance the checkbook! Conversely many women do yard work, mow the lawn, prune/trim bushes, plant gardens, and wash the car! If you plan to immigrate to the United States, plan to become familiar with daily routines! Working in the yard, kitchen and household chores are perennial obligations! Do not let your gender dictate any of the above functions! You will enjoy the benefits, convenience, and savings! We have listed a few helpful tips for you to better cope with living in the United States. Developing some of these skills is a MUST if you are to enjoy your stay in the United States.

Food, Finances, And Transport— Recommendations And Tips:

- You must eat to live! Therefore make a point to learn basic cooking. A cook must shop for ingredients for his/her specialized cooking. Most stores/markets in almost all cities in the United States carry foods and delicacies from all over the world. Grocery store clerks are courteous and ready to help you. Just ask.
- The microwave is essential for everyday cooking in the United States. Most homes have this necessary appliance. A microwave is a convenience to people with a busy schedule.
- Certain foods especially spices, tend to fill the air with aromas. Remember to turn on the exhaust fan so your house/ apartment does not suffocate your guests and neighbors.
- It's very important that you become familiar with kitchen and household chores such as cooking, garbage removal, laundry, and maintenance of appliances. Modern conveniences and readily available tools make most of these chores a pleasant experience!

- Almost all women as well as men manage all their business and personal affairs. Banking and investments included! You owe it to yourself to become familiar with this aspect of living. Managing finances and promptly paying bills help improve your credit – a valuable asset!

- A Bank account with a credit card is essential. All your bills must be paid by checks, credit/debit card or a draft. A bank account will help you to develop and build your credit history. Your borrowing power is based on your credit worthy status. As much as situations permit do not carry excess cash. Cash is easily stolen or lost! When you pay cash for large purchases, returning the merchandise may be cumbersome therefore always insist on paying by credit card.

- A driver's license is a MUST in America. It offers you freedom! You will be able to report to work or school on time all the time. However owning and operating an automobile requires mandatory liability insurance, fuel, maintenance, and at times costly repairs.

- Most cities in the United States have adequate mass transit such as trains, subway systems, bus, and cab service. You may need a cab for special occasions - call for this service at least 1-2 hours ahead. Inform the cab service where you are currently located, where you need to go, and how many in your party. A courteous cab driver deserves a decent tip!

- Carry your picture identification (ID) at all times. The banks, local, state, and federal offices will require your picture ID to process your requests. All federal, state, and some local buildings require a picture ID to enter the premises! If you do not have a picture identification bring your passport.

- Every legal immigrant in America MUST have a Social Security Number (SSN). Visit the nearest Social Security Office to apply for your Social Security Card. Remember to carry it with you at all times.

It's impossible to deal with every aspect of American living in a Guide such as this. Every community/neighborhood in America is unique and offers special opportunities. Make time to visit the nearest library to learn much about the community you reside in. Educate yourself about the people, places, and events in and around your neighborhood. Know the parks, museums, and other places of attraction the community is famous for. You may also have many other interests requiring for you to go beyond your community. If you are free to travel, make time to visit places of your choice, explore, and enjoy to your heart's content! Every day 24/7 neighborhood/community publications, daily newspapers, radio, and television will bring you current events and breaking news about your community and surrounding neighborhoods. Learn more about the United States and your community from the media and from your own explorations. You will find yourself in good company with millions of Americans!

CHAPTER THIRTEEN
SELECT IDIOMS, EXPRESSIONS, SLANG, AND CLICHÉS

The primary goal of this Guide is to develop a bridge of understanding that will lead you to greater insights and appreciation of American society, culture, business, and education. In this chapter we provide you with an additional tool and valuable resource. We will fine-tune you to complex American vocabulary, local expressions, slang, and clichés. The power of eloquent expression, ability to grasp unspoken, hidden, and implied meaning of a conversation will enhance your ability to deal with complex situations, a huge advantage in this modern American society.

American English language has a rich collection of phrases, idioms, slang, and cliché's that may at first almost overwhelm you. But if these phrases and idioms are used in the right context at the right time they deliver a very powerful message by going beyond the literal meaning of the words. The meaning of such phrases may be intended to communicate a point of view, point out the reality of a situation, clear the air, or reiterate a strong position that an individual has on a specific issue dear to his/her heart. Some of the phrases, idioms, and cliché's are routinely used for humor. More often than not such expressions are used to caution, warn, and deliver back-handed advice! Not knowing these phrases and the context in which they are best used may severely restrict your understanding of the true meaning of the conversation you carry on. Some of these phrases are symbolic or figure of speech that has illustrative meanings. Making yourself familiar with these phrases, slang, and clichés will enhance your ability to comprehend the gut of a conversation or humor fully.

Whenever you hear a phrase that makes no sense literally, you will know that it is an idiom, phrase or a cliché. The following pages have a list of carefully selected such frequently used terms, phrases, and expressions. They are listed in alphabetical order for quick reference.

A.

Above board: Honest, fair, and legitimate. Referred to a person of integrity and honesty.

Absence makes the heart grow fonder: If two people such as intimate friends, family members, or lovers are separated due to distance or other barriers, their love for each other grows stronger as a result.

Achilles heel: (Referring to Achilles from Greek mythology) A weakness that makes one vulnerable. Even prominent individuals have an Achilles heel.

Acid test: Confirms a critical fact as true or false beyond a shadow of doubt.

Actions speak louder than words: What you accomplish through deeds is the proof and measure of your integrity/success rather what you claim/say you are.

Add fuel to fire/flames (Add insult to injury): Intentionally aggravate or intensify a situation. Offend someone with hostility.

Air your dirty linen/laundry in public: Humiliate, speak ill of a person in the presence of a large crowd.

All chiefs and no Indians: Situations where too many people issue orders and too few people implement them!

All Ears: Anxious to listen to something important or thought provoking.

All Greek to us (me): Refers to something totally new and foreign. Something that you find difficult to understand.

Alleluia: An exclamation of happiness or praise to God.

Amen: Expression of assent.

Apple of my/your eye: A very special family member, your favorite person.

At my beck and call: Always at your command! Eager to do as requested.

At my wits end: Confused, frustrated, and not knowing what to do next.

Avoid like a plague: Stay away from or avoid a situation/person by all means - even if it is inconvenient!

B.

Backseat Driver: Someone who interferes with the person responsible to get the job done. A passenger attempting to command/teach the operator of a vehicle the art of driving!

Bad news travels fast: Such as gossip. Bad news is interesting!

Baptism by fire: Someone who is instantly challenged on his/her first day on the job or a project (usually with little or no training).

Beat around the bush: Evade, avoid the real issues when confronted.

Beat him/her to the punch: Do something before he/she (friend or foe) can get to it! Beat the adversary by well-conceived tactics, skill and connections.

Beat the rap: Avoid punishment by clever tactics.

Beauty is only skin-deep: Good looks are no guarantee of good character, good judgment, intelligence, and integrity.

Bed of Roses: Very comfortable situation. A wonderful fun filled good life.

Behind the 8-ball: In trouble or in an unpleasant situation.

Better be safe than sorry: A backdoor advice. Go for the safe and sure option rather than invite risk.

Better late than never: It's wise to show up late than not at all!

Between a rock and a hard place: Having to choose between two unfavorable options. A no win situation.

Birds of the feather flock together: People typically associate with others with whom they share common values, interests, and beliefs.

Bite off more than you can chew: Engage in a task that is beyond your ability and expertise to accomplish fully.

Bite the bullet: Accept an unpleasant, difficult situation as a last resort because other options are even less attractive.

Bite the dust: Disappear, die, and be gone.

Bite your tongue: An abrasive way to ask you to be quiet!

Black sheep of the family: A family member or a relative with bad reputation.

Blow it: Miss an opportunity to succeed due to a mistake or a huge error in judgment (both of them could have been avoided).

Blow the whistle: Expose dishonesty to public scrutiny (whistle-blower). An employee or a client who exposes your misdeeds by going public with specific information.

Bolt out of the blue: Unexpected surprise (can be good or bad).

Bone of Contention: A certain issue or a situation that alienates family, friends, neighbors, or business associates.

Bone to pick: A friendly way of expressing one's desire to discuss a dispute or a situation with willingness to compromise and resolve.

Break the ice: Overcome reticence. After a period of initial silence the first one to initiate a conversation breaks the ice.

Bring home the bacon: Engage in a steady paying job to support your family.

Bread-winner: The employed member of the household (husband or wife).

Bury the hatchet: Forget and forgive, make peace, quit being bitter.

C.

Call a spade a spade: Tell it like it is.

Call it a day (call it quits): Stop work or activities either because it is getting late/dark or the project is at a point of convenient stop.

Call the shots: Take control of a project/situation, order employees and subordinates to continue or stop the process.

Catch red-handed: Catch someone in the act! Discover an individual in the process of doing something wrong such as stealing money, valuables, or engage in gossip.

Clear the air: Explain the situation, clear doubt or misunderstanding.

Coast is clear: The danger has been removed. It is OK to engage and continue whatever was started/or was in progress.

Cock and bull story: Untrue, exaggerated story told to build your ego and impress the audience.

Cold Feet: Fear, insecurity, anxiety, doubts, and second thoughts about a project. Fear of failure or heavy loss!

Cold hands, warm heart: Nice way to compliment one who has lots of love and compassion for others.

Cold Shoulder: Ignore/avoid a friend, family member or an acquaintance for a reason.

Come hell or high water: A call to overcome obstacles, work hard, and get the job done.

Cook your goose: Plan and create problems for you as a revenge.

Cool as a cucumber: Calm and composed in spite of problems and difficult situations.

Cough it up: Insist that you pay up the money owed now! Force/insist that you divulge a secret.

Count on: Rely or depend on you for an important event, money or favor.

(The)Cutting Edge: Most current advances in research and technology. Latest innovations, developments, and practices/procedures.

D.

Dawn on: Begin to realize or understand a situation clearly.

Dark horse: One with hidden talents and qualities not expected to win.

Dig your own grave: Unwittingly inviting/causing your own downfall.

Do as I say, not as I do: A sarcastic reminder that your words do not match your deeds!

Dog-eat-dog: Ruthless, brutal competition. Try to win at any cost!

(It's a) Dog's life: A very unhappy, miserable way of living.

Don't count your chickens before they're hatched: It's a warning (advice) not to expect positive results too soon. Don't make plans based on your anticipated positive outcome or illusionary success - be patient!

Down in the dumps: Very unhappy/depressed. In poor financial, psychological, or physical condition.

Down-to-earth: Modest, humble, unpretentious person with good sense.

Drink like a fish: One who habitually consumes large quantities of alcohol is known to drink like a fish.

Drive you up a wall: Cause you to be extremely unhappy and frustrated.

Dutch courage: Unusual courage or aggression exhibited only when intoxicated!

E.

Eager beaver: One who is industrious and ambitious. At times this kind of behavior is deemed inappropriate. Eager beavers tend to be motivated to win praise, money, material, or favors!

Eagle eye: Exceptionally sharp vision or keen perception.

Ear to the ground: Being astute, well informed, and alert.

Easy come, easy go: What is acquired with little or no effort is often lost quickly and easily too.

Eat humble pie: A humiliating experience.

Eat like a horse: Consume large quantities of food.

Egg on one's face (to have): Make a fool of oneself. Invite ridicule!

Egg someone on: Trick someone to do or say something inappropriate.

End of your rope: Stretching all limits of your ability and patience to cope with failure, frustration, and anger.

F.

Faint heart: A weak person who is not able to deal with difficult situations or tough tasks/issues - a coward!

Fair and square: Honest, fair, and truthful individual.

Fall on deaf ears: To ignore or pay no attention.

Feather in your cap: An honor. An accomplishment for which you should be proud.

Fiddle around: Work with no plans, accomplish little or nothing. Waste time.

Fiddle while Rome burns: Acting very busy with insignificant details while important matters being ignored.

Fish out of water: Totally out of place and uncomfortable in a particular situation or environment.

Fit as fiddle: Feeling strong and in robust health.

Flip your lid: Get angry, lose self-control.

Fly off the handle: Get angry instantly for no good/valid reason.

Fly-by-night: Erratic, untrustworthy, and unreliable.

Food for thought: Something worth thinking about (a new idea).

Fool's paradise: Experience happiness based on a false promise or illusion.

Freeload: Live off of others, accept and enjoy things others pay for.

From scratch: Start from the very beginning. When you bake a cake from raw materials or basic ingredients – you are baking a cake from scratch!

G.

Gentleman's agreement: Refers to an unwritten agreement purely based on mutual trust and hand shake.

Get a grip on yourself: It's a backdoor advice imploring you to control your emotions and behave appropriately.

Get a kick out of: Have a spontaneous pleasant experience/surprise with someone's contribution, participation in a project or an event.

Get ahead: Advance or become successful in a business, career or profession.

Get even: Hit back at someone or take revenge for the hurt he/she caused you in the past. Tit for tat!

Get off my back: Leave me alone, quit criticizing and interfering with my business/life. This could be a request or a demand!

Get off the ground: Make a good start.

Get you down: Make you feel depressed, unhappy.

Get your goat: Make you angry, upset, and annoyed.

Get your act together: It's a command! Get yourself organized, plan ahead in order to function efficiently.

Get (sink) your teeth into: Begin to work at something in a determined, aggressive manner with a good plan.

Get out of hand: Lose control of a situation.

Get to the bottom of: Investigate, determine the real cause of failure/ success of a project or an incident.

Get under your skin: Deliberately annoy, harass and upset you!

Gift of the Gab: Ability to talk eloquently and skillfully.

Give in: Surrender or submit to your demands.

Give you a hand: Help, assist you in what you are doing so it will be done quickly.

Give you the slip: Get away from you without your notice!

Go cold turkey: Abruptly stop/quit an addiction such as smoking, alcohol, gambling, or any other illicit activity/bad habit.

Go down swinging: Fight hard until the very end, yet lose.

Go Dutch: Each pays his/her own share for meals, drinks, and entertainment by prearrangement.

Go haywire: Totally erratic uncontrolled behavior.

Go out of your way: Make extraordinary effort to do more than required, expected, and necessary.

Go the extra mile: Spend extra time, money, and effort to get the job done right.

Go to the dogs: Waste, lose value.

Go to bat for: Help, assist, and guide someone in time of need.

Go under the knife: Refers to surgery.

Go getter: Ambitious, aggressive, hard working person usually gets things done.

Goner: Refers to a loser.

Grin and bear it: Accept a difficult, painful proposition against your will because other options are no better!

H.

Hale and hearty: Fit as a fiddle. Refers to your good health.

Half baked: Stupid, foolish, silly person!

Hand over fist: Earn lots of money, accumulate wealth quickly.

Hand to mouth: Barely able to live with the amount of money earned.

Handout: Receive charity such as free food, clothes, money, and material.

Hard and fast: Rules and regulations that cannot be changed for anyone under any circumstances.

Hard up: Destitute, very poor.

Has it made: One who is successful and has all the comforts.

Has no prayer: any chance of success!

Have a ball: Have a good time.

Have a crush on: Romantically attracted.

Have a head on your shoulder: A left handed compliment. You are intelligent and predictable!

Have a mind of your own: Thinking and acting independently. This phrase is most often said to rebuke you because you failed to follow good advice!

Have been around: Experienced, not a novice. Admit that you know what to do.

Have your hand in the till: Caught stealing money or material.

Have something up your sleeves: Scheming! Waiting for the right time and opportunity to execute your (good or bad) plan.

Head Honcho: The person in charge, the boss, the leader.

Heart-to-heart: A confidential, intimate, and honest discussion/ huddle.

Hit below the belt: Intentionally hurt someone (unfairly) with no remorse.

Hit it off with you: To become friends with you fairly fast. To get along well because of good chemistry!

Hit the bottle: Drink excessive alcohol.

Hit the ceiling: Get very angry about a specific situation.

Hit the nail on the head: Have a correct/right solution. Accurately analyses a situation or a problem.

Hit the sack: Go to bed.

Hit the skids: Experience bad times.

Hit the spot: Extremely satisfying and timely - usually referred to an alcoholic beverage or refreshment.

Hogwash: Something that is totally out of line, inaccurate, and untrue.

Hold the fort: Look after business or property while the boss, manager, or partner is away.

Hold your own: Do well in a fight/debate/sport event against tough competition.

Honey catches more flies than vinegar: A left handed advice to be kind and gentle! Good begets good!

Hors d'oeuvre: Appetizers (starters) served before a meal/dinner.

I.

Icon: A hero and a role model. Symbolic of a movement or a good cause.

If you can't stand the heat, stay out of the kitchen: Backhanded advice to accept the responsibilities that go with the job.

Ill-gotten goods never thrive: Wealth acquired by deceit/hook or crook will not last.

Imbroglio: A very confused situation. Complicated affair.

In a bind: In a very difficult situation. In a jam. In hot water.

In a huddle: Confidential meeting, conference, discussion.

In a nutshell: Very briefly and accurately summarized.

In black and white: Have an agreement in writing rather than verbal assurance.

In seventh heaven: Very happy and excited.

In the doghouse: In trouble with spouse or the boss!

In the Klink: In jail/prison.

In the red: When expenses exceed income.

In the same boat: In similar or identical situation.

Iron out: Discuss the differences and resolve issues to mutual satisfaction.

J.

Jack of all trades: Someone who can perform multiple jobs knows a little bit about each but is not a master of any.

Jack up: Raise the price of goods or services without just reason.

Jam-packed: Very crowded.

Jitters: Nervous, anxious, and not too happy.

Jump down your throat: Talk to you with intense anger and hostility.

Jump (hop, get, and climb) on the bandwagon: Join the group/crowd for fun and good times. Join the group for a cause.

Jump to conclusion: Decide/conclude without good understanding of issues.

Jump the gun: Respond without thinking! Come to a conclusion with inadequate evidence or proof.

K.

Keep a low profile: Avoid being noticed. Stay away from the limelight.

Keep a stiff upper lip: Do not show nor share true feelings and emotions.

Keep at arm's length: Maintain distance. Intentionally avoid someone.

Keep your head above water: Manage money so as to be able to pay bills and support your household.

Keep your nose clean: Stay out of trouble.

Keep tabs on: Keep an eye on someone or something out of curiosity or jealousy. This is inappropriate, meddlesome behavior!

Keep the balls rolling: Continue the activity without pause.

Keep up with the Joneses: Try and maintain your lifestyle to match that of your neighbors, friends, and acquaintances.

Keep your chin up: Have courage and move on. Gentle advice not to lose hope.

Kick the bucket: To die.

Kill the goose that lays the golden egg: To bring an end to your benefits by destroying the source - clearly an act of greed!

Kill two birds with one stone: Fulfill/accomplish two goals with one action.

Kiss of death: An act that will bring loss and destruction.

Knock it off: It's an order for you to stop! Discontinue at once whatever activity such as an argument, fight, or horseplay!

Knock one (them) dead: Do a good job and impress everyone.

L.

Land on your feet (fall on your feet): Achieve success after a prolonged struggle and hard work.

Last straw (the last straw that broke the camel's back): Refers to the last minor event in a series of events that causes the unpleasant result.

Lay your cards on the table: Be absolutely truthful regarding your role, motives, and intentions in a dispute/fight. Insist that you come clean!

Learn the ropes: Study and learn all the intricate, fine details of a job or business.

Leave in the lurch: Abruptly leave someone to face a difficult situation.

Leave no stone unturned: Make absolutely sure that all that's needed to be done has been done right.

Let bygones be bygones: Urge one to forget the past differences, make peace, become friends, and move on!

Let's get the show on the road: Implore the gathering or the people in charge of an event such as sport, social function or play, not to delay but get started immediately.

Let the cat out of the bag: Divulge a secret.

Like clockwork: Efficient operation. Applies to business, project, or a social event.

Lion's share: Largest portion of food, money or material.

Lip service: Offer only verbal/oral support - no material help!

Live high off the hog: Life full of luxuries and comforts.

Live it up: Have a good time.

Long shot: Someone who has a slim chance of success.

Lose your marbles: Lose self-control either out of anger or some other reason. It also refers to your irrational behavior or senility!

Lose your shirt: Lose money either by business failure, inviting risks, bad investment, gambling, and the like!

M.

Magna cum laude: With great distinction.

Make a federal case out of: Over react to a minor mischief.

Make hay while the sun shines: Take advantage of an opportunity.

Make a killing: Make huge amounts of money. Refers to a one time gain such as a sale, gambling win or a business transaction.

Make a mountain out of molehill: Exaggerate. Make a big issue out of an insignificant, minor event. Make a federal case!

Make ends meet: Earn barely enough to survive. Live within your means.

Make your hair stand up: Get frightened over something. Feel insecure!

Make or break: Crucial situation that can end in success or utter failure.

Many hands make light work: When many people participate in a project and work as a team, rapid progress is possible.

Man-to-man: Frank, heart-to-heart talk to resolve differences and overcome distrust!

Marry in haste and repent at leisure: A back door advice to be careful.

Midas touch: Ability/skill to make money/succeed in an undertaking.

Mind-boggling: Totally confusing, difficult to comprehend!

Miss the boat: Waste a good chance, miss a fine opportunity to succeed or accomplish your goal.

Mooch: Borrow, beg. Get something without paying for it.

Move heaven and earth: Leave no stone unturned, make extraordinary effort to get the job done!

Mudslinging: Talk ill of a person. Make false statements to hurt one's reputation.

Mum's the word: Code phrase to someone not to divulge a secret.

N.

Name names: Inform authorities the identity of people involved in a crime, disturbance or a conspiracy.

Neat as a pin: Tidy, orderly, and exceptionally clean.

Nest Egg: Money saved for your future such as retirement.

Nincompoop: Incompetent.

Nip in the bud: Kill it off /force an end to a bad habit. Stop a project before it is even started in order to save money and spare discomfort.

Nitpick: Habitually looking for petty mistakes/errors in order to give a hard time to an employee/coworker.

Nitty-gritty: Details of a project or a process.

Nitwit: Refers to an idiot (stupid person).

No spring chicken: A humorous way of implying that you are no longer as young as you look, act or pretend to be.

Nobody's fool: Someone who is intelligent, competent, and well-informed.

Nothing ventured, nothing gained: It's a back door advice to try what is at hand, to get busy, and take some risk in order to succeed.

Nuts about: Madly in love with.

O.

Off base: Not true, inaccurate.

Off your rocker: Crazy, senile.

Off the hook: Out of trouble, cleared from a court case or an issue of bother/discomfort.

Old flame: Former girlfriend, boyfriend or ex-lover.

Old habits die-hard: Refers to bad habits/manners that are hard to break.

On the ball: When you are on top of things, completely in charge, and doing well - you are on the ball!

On the go: Always busy, constantly involved in some activity.

On the gravy train: Someone doing well, making lots of money.

On the house: Food and drinks (snacks/deserts/refreshments) provided free of charge by bars and restaurants as a promotion.

On the level: Truthful, honest.

On the rocks: Refers to troubled marriage or relationship that's on the brink of collapse.

On the same wavelength: People who think alike and communicate well with no disagreements.

On the spot: In an embarrassing, uncomfortable situation.

On the warpath: Acting angrily and confrontationally towards employees, coworkers, or just with anyone!

Out of line: Inappropriate behavior or attitude towards your boss, coworker, neighbor, friend, and even strangers.

Over my dead body: Expressing strong opposition to a plan, idea, proposed project, or anticipated relationship.

Over the hill: Past middle age. Old age. Humorous way to talk about your age.

P.

Pad the bill: Falsify expenses in your favor.

Pain in the neck: Not a happy situation. Someone or something causing discomfort, anger, and frustration.

Parting shot: A distraught, critical final remark made by an angry person on his/her way out (to get even).

Pass the buck: Evade accountability, shift responsibility.

Pat on the back: Praise one's ability and skill approvingly. Compliment for a job well done.

Pay through the nose: Pay more than what service/product is worth.

Penny wise and pound-foolish: Too involved in trivial things and not so attentive to important ones.

Perk up: Polite way of comforting a friend or relative not to get upset or depressed over something. It's a well-meaning, kindly effort to cheer you up!

Picture of health: Ideally fit. Fit as a fiddle!

Piece of cake, (That is a): Easy, pleasant task.

Pie in the sky: Illusion of success. False hope of receiving wealth, promotion, or an important position.

Pin one's hope on: Heavily rely on someone or some event to realize one's wishes and aspirations.

Pin him down: Insist that he be truthful and accept certain terms.

Pink slip: Employment termination notice.

Pitch in: Give a helping hand so the job can be completed quickly and on time.

Play ball: Work as a team. Offer/request helping hand in order to get the project moving.

Play hooky: Absent from work or school without permission.

Play it by ear: Improvise, act according to changing situation/conditions.

Play your cards right: Use your position, relationship, and friendship wisely in order to gain maximum advantage.

Play up to you: Praise, flatter you with ulterior motives.

Play with fire: Invite disaster by being irresponsible and reckless with a task or dealing with a person/situation.

Pro bono: Free legal aid provided to the poor.

Pull a fast one: Swindle, cheat, and deceive someone.

Pull your leg: Play a joke, mischief, trick! Tease you for fun.

Pull something off: Accomplish the impossible. Get a very difficult job done.

Pull the rug out from under: Ruin, destroy someone's plans. Withdraw support at the most critical time to facilitate failure.

Pull the wool over your eyes: Cheat, trick, and deceive.

Put down: Talk ill of someone or something.

Put your foot down: Prevent or initiate an act/process by taking a strong stand.

Put our heads together: Exchange ideas, share thoughts, and develop a good plan in order to get the job done right.

Put up a good front: Pretend to be happy when sad. Mislead or fool people with some ulterior motive.

Q.

Quack: A fake doctor. Someone who claims what he/she is not.

Quick as a flash: Task accomplished much faster than anticipated. Something that happened sooner than anticipated.

Quid pro quo (Latin in origin): This for that. Do and give the same in return, tit for tat.

R.

Rags to riches: A poor man's journey to riches and wealth by hard work and also a stroke of luck.

Rake it in: Refers to one's good luck and success in making a lot of money.

Rat race: Endless struggle, competition, and strife for existence.

Raw deal: Unfair, unjust distribution of wealth among family or partners. Ill-treatment for no apparent good reason such as deny a deserved promotion, increase in pay and the like.

Red Carpet treatment: Grand welcome, a very special treatment for an honored guest.

Red-letter day: A very important, special, and memorable day in the history of a country, community, organization, or an institution.

Red tape: Unnecessary official paper work. Bureaucracy that leads to delays.

Ring a bell: Sounds familiar. Stirs a memory. Reminds you of something from the past!

Rip off: Cheat, swindle, deceive.

Rock the boat (Don't): Don't cause trouble. Don't upset the status quo and disturb the peace.

Rub something in: Constantly reminds someone of mistakes he/she made in order to humiliate him/her in public or in the presence of friends.

Rule the roost: Dominate a group or organization. Play the boss!

Run around in circles: Totally confused. Aimlessly running around - usually getting nothing done!

Run ragged: Run out of steam/energy. Exhausted and frustrated.

S.

See eye to eye: In complete agreement, having the same opinion on issues.

See through: Understand the true character, real nature of someone or something.

Sell yourself short: Under estimate your ability/skill.

Send you packing: Terminate your employment with no notice.

Shape up: Implore someone to behave appropriately.

Shell out: Cough up money. Chide someone to pay up!

Shoot the breeze: Socialize informally. Talk idly, chew the fat.

Short end of the stick: Receive unfair treatment for no apparent reason.

Sink your teeth into: Get down to serious work!

Sink or swim: Make or break, succeed or fail by your own efforts or lack of.

Skeleton in your closet (cupboard): A hidden family secret.

(No)Smoke without fire: Refers to a rumor. Rumors have some merit!

Snowball's chance in hell: Absolutely no chance of success.

Song and dance: Make a silly excuse! Explanation that is clearly unconvincing, designed to mislead.

Sourpuss: Someone who is unhappy and disagreeable.

Spick (spic) and span: Exceptionally clean.

Spill the beans: Divulge a secret.

Stand you up: You fail to attend a previously planned luncheon, dinner, or meeting – with no advance notice! This applies to romantic dates also!

Stand up to someone: Confront someone about an issue/idea with no fear but with a touch aggression/hostility. At times it is considered as a bold move!

Start the ball rolling: Initiate the action. This may apply to work, play, or any planned activity...

Stick your neck out: Take a risk.

Stick to your guns: Stick to your position no matter how unpopular. Be consistent!

(A)Stitch in time saves nine: A timely intervention may save lots of trouble in the long run.

(A) Stolen fruit is sweetest: The joy of having something for nothing!

Straight from the horse's mouth: Information received directly from the person in charge of a project/business.

Strike while iron is hot: Take advantage of an opportunity at hand.

Success has many fathers, while failure is an orphan: Everyone loves to own up success while all will shy away from failure!

T.

Taboo: Behaviors that is culturally and socially unacceptable.

Take a crack at: Make an attempt at or accept a challenge in an event such as sports, entertaining and the like.

Take your hat off to someone: Respect, acknowledge someone for his fine performance/skill

Take you for a ride: Cheat, swindle, deceive.

Take you to the cleaners: Take/steal your belongings such as money, property, and assets by hook or crook.

Take the bull by the horns: Face a situation head on. Handle a difficult, thorny situation with courage.

Take the Fifth: Refuse to testify against yourself in a court of law. Refers to the Fifth Amendment to the United States' constitution.

Take it with a grain of salt: Listen to someone with skepticism.

Talk turkey: Serious discussion about business or family affairs.

There's no fool like an old fool: A sarcastic comment made when an older person misbehaves. Implies that he/she should know better.

Throw cold water on: Discourage you in such a way that you will abandon the planed activity/project.

Throw in the towel: Discontinue, give up the plans, and acknowledge defeat.

Throw your weight around: Use your position to influence an outcome on social, political, and other issues.

Tickled pink: Very happy, delighted.

Tighten your belt: Cut back expenditures. Save money and watch pennies!

Tip of the iceberg: What you know at the time is a very small part of a much larger problem or a situation.

Tip someone off: Secretly warn or inform authorities or adversaries of an impending scandal, violation of law or damaging information about someone.

Toe the line: Observe the law, rules, and guidelines fully.

Tooth and nail: A hard fight, fierce competition.

Top notch: Excellent, superb, the best.

Topsy-turvy: Out of control or in great disarray.

Turn a blind eye: Ignore, deliberately overlook a crime/misdeed.

Turn a deaf ear: Completely ignore, disregard, and pay no attention to.

Turn the corner: Crucial progress in a venture, business, or a project.

Turn the tables on: Put a person in an identical situation, place or position as he/she did to you. Pay back with the same coin.

Two-faced: Untrustworthy, disloyal. Refers to a deceitful person.

U.

Under the table: Money given to a person (unknown to others) as a bribe or gift in return for favor(s).

Under the weather: Not feeling well, ill, indisposed.

Up your sleeve, (to have something): Guarding a secret to use against someone (friend or foe) at an opportune time either to blackmail or demand special favor(s).

Up to my ears: Heavily involved and very busy with a planned event/ project. This applies to someone with heavy debts also.

Up to scratch (snuff, par): An applicant for a job/studies/training who meets required standards and qualifications.

Upset the applecart: Spoil a plan. Disturb the planned program/ activities.

V.

Variety is the spice of life: Someone with many interests is more apt to enjoy life, have more fun than those with limited interests.

Vicious circle, A: A continuous, automatic chain reaction that produces a bigger or equally serious problem when the original problem is resolved.

Vigilante: A self-appointed policeman, judge, and administrator of justice.

W.

Walk all over you: Use, exploit or take advantage of your weakness.

Walk on air: Very happy, excited.

Watch (mind) your P's and Q's: A left handed advice to behave appropriately, mind your manners, and be polite!

Wear the pants (trousers): A left handed advice to someone to play the boss and take charge of an event or a situation.

Wedlock is a padlock: Marriage - something that's deemed permanent.

Wet behind the ears: Person with little or no experience.

When the cat's away, the mice will play: When the boss/manager is away the employees will misbehave, disregard rules, and hardly work.

When the chips are down: Unusually difficult financial situation, tough times!

When the wine is in, wit is out: A sarcastic way to refer to someone who carries on a foolish conversation after a few drinks.

Wild goose chase: Wasting time by pursuing wrong ideas and issues.

Wisecrack: Unkind, sarcastic, and nasty remarks made to upset you!

Y.

You can't teach an old dog new trick: An older person with set ways will not listen/adapt to new ideas and therefore may not be taught.

You can't win them all: A resigned, philosophical way of accepting failure or defeat.

Z.

Zero hour: Exact starting time for a game, function, or a party

CHAPTER FOURTEEN
IMMIGRATION ISSUES AND SUGGESTIONS

Non-Immigrant Visas

This concluding chapter has valuable information for you. You have studied, restudied, debated, and decided to immigrate to the United States. You also know the category you belong in for this exciting journey of your lifetime! Now is the time to develop a sound plan for action and implement the same with total discipline. As you prepare to sink your teeth into this process, make a list of DOCUMENTS such as your passport, birth certificate, marriage certificate, diplomas from high school and college, and certificates that list your training and special skills. You may also need financial sponsorship letters, official bank affidavits confirming funds available, and other records to support your travel. All these critically important papers must be legible and current. If the documents are in your local language, the American consulate may request translated, notarized copies in English!

If your visit is for medical reasons, you may be required to produce letter (s) from your physician (s). Qualifying Refugees also need to do additional homework to produce required proof to support their claim (s). Your country of birth may also have special guidelines, such as security clearance and the like. If you find this process too much for you, engage reputable professionals to assist you.

Your final most important step is to secure YOUR VISA to the United States. You must have the visa stamped on your passport to gain entry to the United States. Some countries are partners in a Visa Waiver Program with the United States. If you are a citizen of one of those countries, you do not require a visa – all you need is a valid E-passport to be admitted to the United States! Therefore we recommend that you log on to the State Department's web-site (www.state.gov) to confirm that your country participates in this program. Click on Visa Waiver Program (VWP) for list of countries whose citizens are allowed entry to the United States without visa. But these nationals must have a valid E-passport and all other required documents. These must be presented to the immigration officer at the port of entry to the United States.

If you are not a citizen of one of the visa waived countries, the purpose of your visit will determine the classification of visa you will receive. When planning your visit to the United States, know that there are visa guidelines and pre-requisites for every category - Visa classifications are available from A-1 to WT! You must check with United States Citizenship and Immigration Services (USCIS) for specific information that is applicable to your category. Be sure to inform USCIS the precise reason for your visit and the duration of your stay so they may guide you appropriately. USCIS will also mail you desired information upon request. During your initial contacts, keep in mind the broad categories listed below and inform USCIS the specific category you belong in.

- Students (graduate, post graduate) and Au pairs.
- Professionals, trainees, and employees.

- Investors, business people, and service providers.
- Visitors, temporary stay, medical treatment.
- Tourists, explorers, nature lovers.
- Refugees, asylum seekers or Asylees.

The above categories have well defined specific requirements to secure visa to the United States. You must obtain all the documents required by the American consulate in your country – no exception please! In addition, you may also have to provide proof of income, assets and available funds to support yourself and your family. When you have all these documents and your portfolio is ready – go on line and make that appointment for your visa interview. Your hard work will pay off when you confidently appear to face the consulate officer at the nearest American embassy!

Your personal interview will be short and sweet – the interviewing officer will inform you that your request for visa application is granted! Your passport with visa stamped on it will be mailed to you within a few days – all you have to do is wait for the pleasant delivery and use this time to shop around for the best air-fare to the city of your destination in the United States!

Not all aspiring immigrants are issued visas – some may have to try again with additional supporting documents and some others may have to wait! It's important for you to know that as a matter of procedure, American Embassy personnel view all visa applicants to be harboring other plans! Therefore it's incumbent upon you to make your case, gain trust, and build confidence in your interviewing officer. He/she should have no doubts about your intentions to accomplish your stated goals and return to your homeland!

USCIS provides several humanitarian programs to citizens of other countries. Protection to individuals from their own government is offered in some countries! Refugees are provided shelter or aid from disasters. Assistance for emergency medical care and for urgent life-threatening circumstances is also available. You may be required to travel to the United States if you qualify!

American law grants refugee status to people of certain countries who are persecuted for reasons such as race, religion, nationality, ethnicity, and political views. Refugees or their relatives (husband/wife/children) are invited to apply to USCIS to start this process by completing Form I-730. For more information please visit www.uscis.gov. The asylees are allowed to pursue their profession or acquire special skills in their selected profession in the United States. However the asylees must prove their case with supporting documents in order to apply for travel authorization to enter the United States.

Students as a group are ill-prepared to answer some of the critical questions during the interview process. All students seeking Student Visa (F1) must be prepared to demonstrate the following:

- You are officially enrolled for full time studies for the duration of your stay in the United States. You must show proof of credit hours you have registered and anticipated month/year of your graduation.
- You have sufficient funds available for tuition and living expenses. You must present a credible funding plan for the duration of your studies with evidence of support from sponsors and letters from financial institution(s).
- You must demonstrate to the interviewing officer's satisfaction your intent to return to your homeland upon graduation. This may involve job offers, business opportunities, or family commitments in your country.

Visa applicants from third world countries such as Bangladesh, China, India, Indonesia, Malaysia, Mexico, and several others obviously have a tough job! Citizens of these under-developed countries come to the United States for higher studies but seek job opportunities and permanent residency. This is a cause of concern to the United States government! If you are a citizen of any of the above listed or under-developed country, make time and effort to explain your situation to the interviewing officer. Make absolutely certain that he/she is well informed about your plans – your extra hard work and patience will pay off. You may bring information such as letter (s) indicating job offers - most preferably signed by company official (s) on company stationery (letterhead) or proposed plans for investment opportunities. If you have personal or family obligations and financial commitments in your homeland, bring appropriate documents to support your case. This may include bank loans, property transfer, or inheritance issues. If matrimony is on the horizon, provide proof of marriage proposal – include photo album if available!

The American Embassy provides guidance sheets for all visa applicants for all categories. If you are a student (Visa-Class F or M), student's spouse, or belong to other categories, request for updates and most current information in your category. Please pay close attention to all listed requirements; it is important that you do!

Instructions For Students And Their Dependents

Guidance Sheet For Student Visa (Classes F or M) Interview:

- Passport, Visa fee receipt, and appointment letter. Student and Exchange Visitor Information System (SEVIS) generated original Form I-20, approved and signed by authorized person in charge of foreign students at college or university.

- Proof of payment of SEVIS Fee Receipt I-901, if applicable.
- Evidence supporting financial resources. Acceptable bank statements, proof of liquid assets, and readily available funds to support studies for the duration of student life. Scholarship and assistance offers must be included!
- Original School Transcripts such as degree/diploma certificate and score cards. Certificate (s) to show training and special skills.
- Letter from the sponsor. Sponsor's income (supported by tax returns) and bank statements signed by the Bank Manager.
- All relevant test scores such as TOEFEL, SAT, GRE, GMAT or LSAT.

Guidance Sheet For Student's Spouse And Dependents:

- Passport, visa fee receipt, and appointment letter.
- Individual (personal) original I-20 approved and signed by the Foreign Student Advisor of the college or university. A notarized copy may be acceptable, be sure to confirm!
- A copy of the I-20 for each applicant (spouse & children).
- Photocopy of the Principal Applicant's (spouse/children) valid visa number (if applying separately).
- Original marriage certificate and the entire wedding picture album.
- Original Birth certificate (s) for children.
- Evidence of additional financial resources to support dependent children.

You may enlist a sponsor and provide required supporting evidence as described above.

Visa requirements are subject to change without notice. You may get updated information by visiting www.vfs-usa.co.in before your personal interview at the American Embassy in your homeland. You will save much time and inconvenience!

Visa approval to other categories is just as stringent as above, therefore it's wise to pay careful attention to all details and present your case in a thorough, truthful, and consistent manner. Please follow instructions from appropriate links from USCIS home page.

Student (F1) visa classification has certain restrictions, especially if you seek employment. On campus work is permitted for foreign students by USCIS regulations. Off Campus work is allowed only if the employer has filed a labor petition. H-1B workers must receive a job-specific visa and may only be paid by the company that sponsored them. H-4 visa is for dependents of some other visa holders (H-1A, H-1B, H-2A, H-2B or H-3). These dependents are not allowed employment or to receive payments from any source in the United States. Always keep in mind your special visa classification as referred to in the Employment Authorization Document (EAD).

Asylum applicants, asylees/refugees, pending immigrants, permanent residents, temporary residents, and conditional residents may be issued a voucher or permit for employment. Undocumented aliens who enter the United States illegally and immigrants who no longer enjoy legal status are not eligible for employment. Hundreds of these aliens or illegal immigrants (as they are referred to) are routinely rounded up and imprisoned by the law enforcement agencies in several states! Thousands of students and visitors engaged in unauthorized employment are deported routinely! The federal and state governments have zero tolerance for illegal immigrants and undocumented aliens, it is more so since 9/11.

By carefully adhering to specific guidelines provided by USCIS, you may apply and legally change your residency status in the United States. The USCIS welcomes inquiries from all prospective applicants. Therefore always rely on USCIS for accurate, authoritative information. You may also contact and engage reputable legal service for all your immigration needs - you will be glad you did!

For purposes of greater clarity and convenience you must visit the United States Citizenship and Immigration Services' (USCIS) website. The home page will guide you well on all immigration and naturalization matters. Once you know the category you are qualified for, click on the link and proceed to obtain information that applies to your personal/family situation. Make yourself very familiar with immigration and naturalization requirements by reading and rereading some of the hot topics. If you must seek legal or professional counsel, consult only such services that are appropriate to your special category by doing diligent home work. The USCIS may have an approved list of professional services. Request and obtain that list and get a head start!

APPENDIX

American Big Cities And Attractions
World-Famous Universities And Colleges
Our National Anthem

This resource section will provide useful additional general information for you. We have listed some of America's most interesting places of attraction such as major cities, national parks, natural unique wonderlands, national monuments, historical sites, outstanding universities, and prestigious colleges. The list is by no means complete. There are hundreds of other cities, places, parks, and exciting tourist gold mines not listed here. You may wish to visit many of these according to your convenience, personal preference, or professional interests.

The short list of large cities is just the beginning. Almost all large and not so large cities in the United States have many outlets for fun, recreation, sports, and other activities. In some cities you will find multiple events taking place simultaneously. Cities, communities, and church groups organize festivals (spring or fall), food tasting events, and many outdoor and indoor programs all year round. Americans in particular look forward to spring, summer, and fall seasons for outdoor fun and excitement. Various seasonal and community events, church festivals, and school functions are organized with a great deal of fanfare. All such occasions are operated by community, church, and school leaders with abundant supply of food and refreshments. They organize games, musicals, shows, and wide range of pure fun filled competitions for men, women, and children. Local musician groups provide entertainment for all! Valentine's day, Mother's day, Memorial day, Father's day, Independence day, Labor day, Thanksgiving, Christmas, and New years' day are special holidays. Most Americans make elaborate plans for these occasions and look forward to meeting family and friends! My most memorable and special occasions in the United States has always been Thanksgiving and Christmas. Visiting with my favorite friends and families, exchanging hugs and gifts is great fun. During this brief season, you will most certainly experience extraordinary excitement, much Christmas joy, and endless festivities – a proud tradition in the United States that you will not forget!

Almost all the major cities in the United States aggressively cater to the needs, comforts, and interests of tourists. City governments and affiliates make great effort to attract and entertain visitors to their cities and communities. Therefore, you will find the following facilities always available to you.

- Tourist Information signs posted in convenient locations.
- Hundreds of hotel and motel rooms available to accommodate tourists and visitors. Be sure to reserve your room(s) well in advance.
- Many kinds of museums (such as museum of art, history, science, sports, and technology) always eager to welcome you.

- State-of-the art modern libraries equipped with computers.
- All types of sports such as baseball, basketball, football, soccer, ice hockey, horse racing, and other events for sports fans.
- National parks, theme parks, water parks, historical monuments of interest for adults and children.
- Aquariums, amusement parks, children's parks, wildlife, zoos, and other places of interest.
- Most cities offer unique local attractions such as live shows, cultural and social events. Check the local city guides, newspapers, radio, and television for current events.

15 Largest Cities Of United States

1. New York City (New York) is the largest city in the United States. It is recognized as one of the world's most important centers of commerce, trade, and culture. United Nations headquarters are located in New York City.

New York City is a tourist's paradise. Each year millions of visitors, business people, entertainers, and artists come to the city for fun, pleasure, business, and diplomatic activity. The city has many kinds of museums, several parks, and many more places of historical interest. The City is also well known for year round live theater and Broadway Shows.

2. Los Angeles (California) is the second largest city in the United States. It is known for cultural life, recreation, trade, and commerce. Los Angeles has some of the finest beaches, museums, historical sites, and of course Hollywood!

Millions of visitors tour Los Angeles each year for fun, pleasure, recreation, and business. The scenic city offers great outdoor life. The year round mild temperatures and pleasant climate make LA a popular and enjoyable destination.

3. Chicago (Illinois) is the third largest U.S. city located in the Midwest. Chicago has the world's largest grain market, leading medical facilities, industry, and some of the world's tallest buildings. Chicago attracts millions of tourists and business people each year. The city has world famous museums, parks, and much more. The coastline of Lake Michigan adds beauty and serenity to the city.

4. Houston (Texas) is a modern and vibrant city in the Southwest. Like New York and Los Angeles, Houston has a busy seaport. It is a leading cultural, commercial, and educational center. Houston's attractions include Lyndon B. Johnson Space Center, Texas Medical Center, several museums, parks, and modern libraries.

5. Philadelphia (Pennsylvania) is famously known as the birthplace of the United States of America. The Declaration of Independence and the United States' Constitution were signed in the city's historic Independence Hall. Philadelphia attracts millions of tourists every year. Visitors enjoy history, culture, music, museums, parks, and much more in this majestic historic city.

6. Phoenix (Arizona) is the 6th largest city in the United States. The mild climate has helped Phoenix develop into a major winter resort. Phoenix is also a huge manufacturing center. People visit this city for good weather, the outdoor life, pleasure, recreation, and business.

7. San Antonio (Texas) is a historic city. It has large military bases, many attractive parks, educational institutions, museums, and an active tourism industry. Millions of tourists visit scenic San Antonio for recreation and business.

8. San Diego (California) is the 8th largest city in the United States. San Diego has the world famous Zoo and Sea World. It is also well known for cultural life, museums, libraries, and much more. Millions visit San Diego for fun, pleasure, outdoor life, and business.

9. Dallas (Texas) is the third largest city in Texas. Dallas is the financial capital of Southwest. The city is known for insurance, transportation, and manufacturing industry. Dallas has many museums, parks, and many places of interest for visitors and tourists. Dallas attracts a large number of convention tourists, visitors, and

business people throughout the year. The year round pleasant climate is also a consideration. President John F. Kennedy was shot and killed in Dallas.

10. San Jose (California) is the third largest city in California. The San Jose area is known as Silicon Valley. Products for computers, electronics, and semiconductor industries are the primary sources of revenue and employment in San Jose. Tourists and business people come to San Jose for fun, outdoor life, recreation, and business.

11. Detroit (Michigan) is the largest city in Michigan. It's the automobile capital of the world and is fondly known as Motor City (Mo Town). Detroit is a leading manufacturer of heavy machinery, hardware, plumbing fixtures, and chemicals. Detroit offers rich recreation, fun, and cultural activities to tourists, visitors, and business people.

12. Indianapolis (Indiana) is the largest city and capital of Indiana. It is centrally located and has a strong manufacturing and distribution base. The city is only a few hundred miles south of Chicago. Indianapolis also has many museums, several parks, and historic places. Indianapolis is known for the world famous annual Indy 500 auto racing event.

13. Jacksonville (Florida) is the largest city in Florida. This port city is a leader in the insurance, finance, distribution, and transport industries. It is also home for many parks and recreational facilities. Tens of thousands of tourists and business people visit Jacksonville each year for good weather, fun, and recreation.

14. San Francisco (California) is a beautiful port city on the Pacific coast. The landscape, hills, valleys, parks, museums, scenic view, and pleasant climate make it a favorite world class tourist destination. The Golden Gate Bridge and the San Francisco Bay area are special attractions. From all over the world, people flock to San Francisco for fun, recreation, and business. San Francisco is also famous for entertainment, food, and refreshments.

15. Columbus (Ohio) is the largest city in the state of Ohio. It is also the capital of the state. Columbus has one of the nation's largest universities - The Ohio State University. Columbus has numerous parks, museums, and many places of attraction for fun and recreation.

The National Park System was established for the benefit of all Americans. The goal was to preserve large areas of wilderness, unique natural wonderlands, historic monuments, battlefields, and historic buildings for present and future generations of Americans.

Natural Parks (Wonderlands)

- Death Valley National Park is located in the states of California and Nevada. It has the lowest land surface in the western hemisphere. This desert land is known for attractive volcanic rock formations.
- Everglades National Park is located in Florida. The park is known for its' subtropical wilderness and wildlife.
- Mammoth Cave National Park is located in central Kentucky. The park surrounds the Mammoth Cave, the world's longest known cave. The other two cave systems, Floyd Collins Crystal Cave and the Flint Ridge Cave are part of the entire cave systems. Explorers discovered a connection between Mammoth Cave and the Flint Ridge Cave system in 1972.

Mammoth Cave is also known as one of the wonders of the Western Hemisphere. The cave contains many lakes, rivers, and waterfalls. Blind fish, beetles, and crayfish live in Echo River, one of the largest rivers of the cave systems. Unique small brown bats are natural inhabitants of Mammoth Cave. The park attracts millions of visitors and explorers each year.

Mammoth Cave - Kentucky

http://www.nationalparkreservations.com/images/mammothcave/mammoth_cave.jpg 3/4/2009

- Redwood National Park in California has some of the world's tallest trees. Thousands of tourists, nature lovers, explorers, and hikers visit Redwood National Park each year.

Redwood Forest - California

Redwood Forest - California

- Yellowstone National Park was established in 1872. The park covers 2,219,791 acres of wilderness in the states of Idaho, Montana, and Wyoming. Yellowstone Park is known for natural wonders such as geysers, hot springs, waterfalls, deep gorges, pristine lakes, and wide variety of wildlife.
- Yosemite National Park is located in east central California. The huge park is famous for scenic mountains, high waterfalls, deep gorges, and gigantic rock formations.

National Memorials

- Lincoln Memorial, built to honor President Abraham

Lincoln, was dedicated to the Nation in 1922. It is located in Washington, D.C. Millions visit the beautiful, majestic historic monument every year.

- Mount Rushmore, located in South Dakota. It is a popular tourist attraction. This mountain has been carved to depict the heads of four famous American presidents. Carved from the granite cliff are the likenesses of George Washington, Thomas Jefferson, Theodore Roosevelt, and Abraham Lincoln.

Mount Rushmore – South Dakota

Mt. Rushmore -South Dakota

- The Statue of Liberty is the best known national monument in the United States. It is also one of the largest statues ever built. The "Lady Liberty" stands tall holding her famous torch on Ellis Island in New York Harbor.

- Vietnam Veterans Memorial was built to honor the brave men and women who fought in the Vietnam War. This is one of the newest memorials and is located in Washington, D.C.
- Washington Monument was built in Washington, D.C. in memory and honor of the Father of our nation, the first Commander-in-Chief, George Washington.

National Military Parks

- Gettysburg, Pennsylvania, where one of the most famous battles of the Civil War was fought. Historians consider this battle to be the turning point of the Civil War. President Abraham Lincoln delivered his famous Gettysburg address here on Nov. 19, 1863.

Natural Wonders

- Niagara Falls: Huge waterfalls on the Niagara River in New York that border United States and Canada. Millions of tourists visit the spectacular mist making falls each year. The Niagara River splits to create two falls, the American Falls on the American side and Horseshoe Falls on the Canadian side. The four observation towers built for tourist's convenience provide great views of the fall.

Man-Made Wonders

- Walt Disney Company developed theme parks for popular entertainment. One such park, Disneyland Resort in Anaheim, California, is a huge tourist attraction. Walt Disney World Resort with the Magic Kingdom, near Orlando, Florida, is yet another favorite tourist destination.

Millions visit these Theme Parks year round. These theme parks are popular with children and young adults.

Niagara Falls – New York

Niagara Falls - New York

Niagara Falls : The Natural Wonder

American Universities And Colleges

The educational system in the United States is the envy of the world. Tens of thousands of students from all over the world study in American universities and colleges. The number of foreign students attending American Educational Institutions has steadily increased in recent years.

Colleges and universities in the United States are identified as (1) operated and administered by private sponsorship, and those (2) operated by public sponsorship such as federal, state, and local governments. Most private schools may be church-related or non-denominational and heavily depend on student fees, endowments, donations, and gifts for their operating income. Public institutions are also supported by these methods but primarily depend on taxes (local & state) for their operating budget.

Colleges and universities in the United States are accredited by one or more accrediting agencies. There are six such regional accrediting authorities in the country. Schools are judged by criteria such as staff and teaching standards, student achievement, equipment, and financial status. As a prospective student, you should know the current standing of the institution you intend to attend.

Some Outstanding Universities And Colleges

National universities offer a wide array of undergraduate and graduate programs. The school's curriculum is outlined in the catalog of the institution. You will find a complete list of courses offered and requirements for such courses in the catalog. Master's and doctoral programs are also offered in various fields along with independent research. Liberal Arts colleges mostly specialize in undergraduate studies. The programs are developed to prepare students for graduate programs and higher education. These colleges provide intense counsel and personal attention to students. Unlike National universities, liberal arts colleges are smaller and offer lower student/teacher ratios and are a major contributing factor for students' high achievement.

Ten Best National Universities (2009)

1. Princeton University- New Jersey
2. Harvard University – Massachusetts
3. Yale University – Connecticut

4. Stanford University – California
5. California Institute of Technology – California
6. University of Pennsylvania – Pennsylvania
7. Massachusetts Institute of Technology – Massachusetts
8. Duke University – North Carolina
9. Columbia University – New York
10. University of Chicago – Illinois

Ten Best Liberal Arts Colleges (2009)

1. Pomona College – California
2. Davidson College – North Carolina
3. Haverford College – Pennsylvania
4. Williams College – Massachusetts
5. Amherst College – Massachusetts
6. Swarthmore College – Pennsylvania
7. Wellesley College – Massachusetts
8. Carleton College - Minnesota
9. Middlebury College – Vermont
10. Bowden College- Maine

Our National Anthem

The "Star-Spangled Banner" is America's National Anthem. Francis Scott Key wrote the lines in 1814. Congress officially approved it in 1931. The United States' National Anthem is recited before public functions, sports cum community events, and most celebrations nationwide.

O say, can you see, by the dawn's early light,

What so proudly we hail'd at the twilight's last gleaming?

Whose broad stripes and bright stars, thro' the perilous fight,

O'er the ramparts we watch'd, were so gallantly streaming?

And the rockets' red glare, the bombs bursting in air,

Gave proof thro' the night that our flag was still there.

O say, does that Star - Spangled Banner yet wave

O'er the land of the free and the home of the brave?

SELECTED REFERENCES

1. Alesi, G. (2008). Barron's U.S. Citizenship Test. 7th Edition.

2. Althen, G. (2003). American Ways: A Guide for Foreigners in the United States. 2nd Edition. Intercultural Press Inc., Yarmouth, Maine, 04096.

3. Carnegie, D., (1998). How To Win Friends and Influence People, Revised Edition. Simon & Schuster, Rockefeller Center, 1230 Avenue of the Americas, New York, NY 10020.

4. Gains, B.K. (1986). Idiomatic American English. Kodansha America International, Distributed by Kodansha America Inc., 575 Lexington Avenue, New York, NY 10022.

5. Johnston, D.B. (2002). Speak American: A Survival Guide to the Language and Culture of the U.S.A. Random House, New York, NY.

6. Kimmel, B.B., & Lubiner, A.M. (2006). Citizenship Made Simple: An Easy-to- read guide to the U.S. citizenship process. Chester, NJ.

7. National Geographic Society (U.S.) (2009). National Geographic Guide to the National Parks of the United States, Washington D.C.: National Geographical Society.

8. Reader's Digest (U.S.) (1993). Discovering America's Past. The Reader's Digest Association Inc. Pleasantville, New York.

9. Tuckerman, N. and Dunnan, N. (1995). The Amy Vanderbilt Complete Book of Etiquette. Bantam Doubleday Dell Publishing Group, Inc. New York, NY 10036.

10. USCIS: U.S. Citizenship and Immigration Services. (2006). Welcome to the United States: A Guide for New Immigrants. Rev. 09/07. Published by United States Department of Homeland Security.

ABOUT THE AUTHOR

Arthur D'Souza owned and operated a very successful clinical diagnostic laboratory in Cincinnati, Ohio. Prior to establishing this state-of-the art automated facility, Dr. D'Souza was a Laboratory Director, providing technical consulting, quality control guidelines, routine operational and logistic support to a large Independent Physician Group Laboratory in upstate New York.

He earned his Ph.D. in 1973, and joined Dr. Gilbert Schiff's research team as a Research Associate at Gamble Research Institute, Cincinnati, Ohio. As a Research Associate, he participated in Public Health projects in Infectious and Communicable diseases of viral origin. During his graduate studies he was employed as a Laboratory Technologist in several greater Cincinnati area hospital laboratories.

Dr. D'Souza is currently retired and resides with his wife Margaret in Amberly Village, a suburb of Cincinnati. "I love landscaping, gardening, growing fruits and vegetables. As a family we take long drives to sample different kinds of food, especially German, Italian and Mexican."

Arthur H. D'Souza

ABOUT THE CO-AUTHOR

Ken Brand, second generation of German immigrants, was raised on a small farm near Indianapolis, Indiana, in the American heartland. He has a BA in Philosophy from St. Joseph's College, Indiana and a M.S. from the University of Dayton, Ohio. He Completed Post Masters Internship in Law from Indiana University and Doctoral Residency from University of Cincinnati, Ohio.

Ken has taught in schools in the states of Indiana, Louisiana, and Ohio. He was Principal of schools in Louisiana and Ohio. He retired from active education in 1992 after 25 years as Principal of Reading Central Schools in Reading, Ohio. Subsequently he worked in Prison ministry and was President of Hand-in-hand Ministries, Inc. He was Editor and Publisher of the National Prisoner Magazine, The Christian Express. Throughout his life he has been a volunteer and leader in numerous youth, civic, community, and church activities.

Ken and his wife Marilyn, live in Finny town, a suburb of Cincinnati. He enjoys his retired life with his wife and grandson Tyler.

Kenneth Brand

Arthur D'Souza

Dear Readers,

We invite you to contact us with your thoughts, comments, and suggestions regarding this Guide.

Thank you,

Arthur D Souza & Ken Brand

arthur_dsouza@msn.com

"A practical Guide written by a no-nonsense successful businessman and entrepreneur, who left Mumbai 45 years ago to get an education and seek fortune in the United States of America. This is the kind of book Arthur D' Souza many years ago wished he had read before arriving in the USA, with less than seven dollars in his pocket."

Phil Paradis

"This is a very helpful Guide for high school and college students. A must read for Job seekers, professionals, and entrepreneurs. We need three for sure."

Chris & Carl

"An Absolute Must Guide for students, visitors, and all who love America, the place you wanna be!"

Larry D'Souza

www.ingramcontent.com/pod-product-compliance
Lightning Source LLC
Chambersburg PA
CBHW030311290526
45785CB00001B/300